powerless point

A Caprice Reader

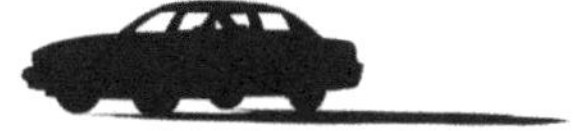

CAPRICE BOOKS

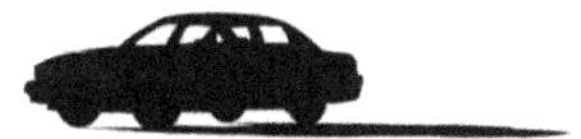

Published by Caprice Books
San Francisco, CA, U.S.A.

For more information regarding any of the work in this book you may contact the publisher here:

capricebooks@gmail.com

Reply, if any, will be slow.

Printed on planet Earth.

powerless point
Caprice Reader № 2
ISBN 978-0-9849159-3-4

Visit Caprice Books on the web:
capricebooks.blogspot.com

Do not expect much.

To the beautiful.

Contents

POETRY

INK (1.)

ESSAY

I N K (2.)

F I C T I O N

The first half of this is by Phillip Levine, a poet in Woodstock, NY, whom I used to know a little. His poem, that he recited in a pub and that I never learned the title to, just delighted me and ran through my head for ages. Its rhythm was in my mind when I wrote **There** *for my wife, Debi. Debi had been feeling powerless about her insomnia and then discovered that meditation helped her...and largely due to that she got over the insomnia completely during a period of two or three years. I was blown away with admiration. To be together for 30 years and be blown away with new respect is deeply double sweet.*

– Dave Belden

Art won't fix it.
Education won't fix it.
The economy won't fix it.
Religion won't fix it.
Therapy won't fix it.
Capitalism won't fix it.
Socialism won't fix it.
Fortunately
It isn't always broken.
-Phillip Levine

There

A fast car gets you there
A taxi gets you there
A bike gets you there
Running gets you there
Plodding gets you there
Now and then,
Sitting gets you there
fastest of all
-Dave Belden

"Sister, Let Me Tell You of Green Light"
--an open letter to C. Fisher

Oh Christina, I read today in the news that a
father of six discovered he was woman when
admitted to the hospital for stones of the kidney.
I do wonder how rare this is.

I can't stop mulling over the complexities of life
that we always seem to unearth.
Who's in what tomb   Who's in which room

The bottomline handshakes so that *we*
are the conspiracy theorists. We can
read and speculate but we'll never really know
what brings about the cancer - my warped gene,
the abnormal cells, crossing fingers,
warning patrons
not to drink the milk, but we can't say
the air is even safe to breathe.

And then there's our parents, touting
"you turned out okay." We can't tell them
the greens have been sprayed,
the shrimp have no eyes,
the cheese has growth hormones.
Lips sealed. We roll our eyes and send love
in text messages and poems we print
occasional airline tickets
to plant our feet and grin.

Oh Christina, the world is broken. We did this—
as humans, not poets, just gluttonous, greedy
human beings. Trails of dead everything, even
you and I kill trees writing out our burdens, but
this is not the worst of it. I keep thinking for you
Dick Gallup is actually perfect, because I think
he'll listen and heed the warnings and teach you
when to turn a blind eye. For you, I want
Galileo, but our parents may not approve.
They eat the cheese! drink the tonic,
follow commercialism's herding.
What more can we do?

Tonight I am eating almonds and dark chocolate
not reading labels, scanning the ticker of news
on mute. I can't get over *mom robs store at*
knifepoint with infant in tow. Seems we're
breaking the world one generation at a time.
You and I
picking hypotheses, adjusting to parenting
parents, enabling indulgences. Sorting what's
for dinner, turning a blind eye to
parents mending fences on the couch.

-Sunnylyn Thibodeaux

To Wear a Knee Brace

We laughed at you Paul
As you talked tough
Spitting garbage slang
Behind yellow tint eyeglasses
With a knee brace on your leg

We laughed at you Paul
Openly to your face
That sat smug like
Under a flat top
That held your acne scars in place

We pitied you Paul
That morning we heard
You'd heaved an axe
Through the skull
Of your pastor, his wife & cat
And set the house ablaze

And no one's laughing now Paul
In prison with the knee brace
Fastened tightly on your leg

-Joshua Baratz

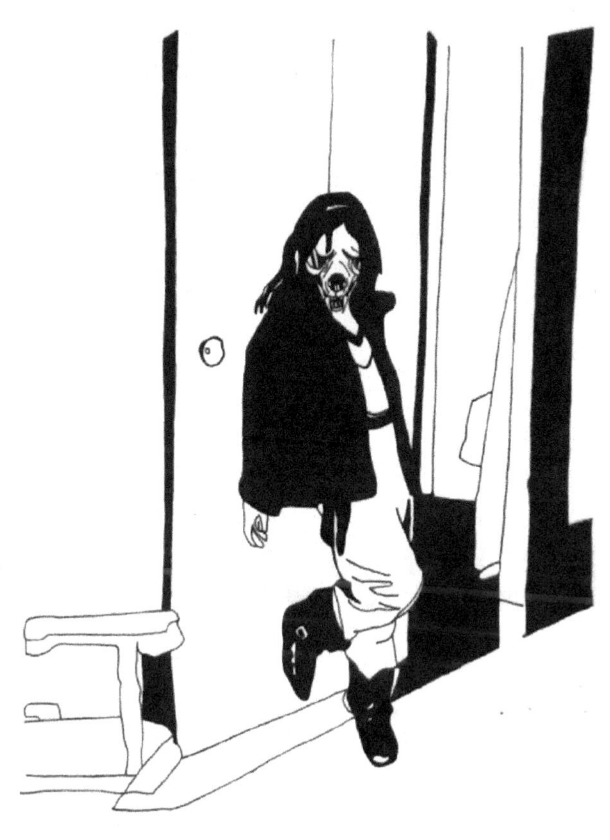

Otter

Rachel Pascua
from the family pictures series

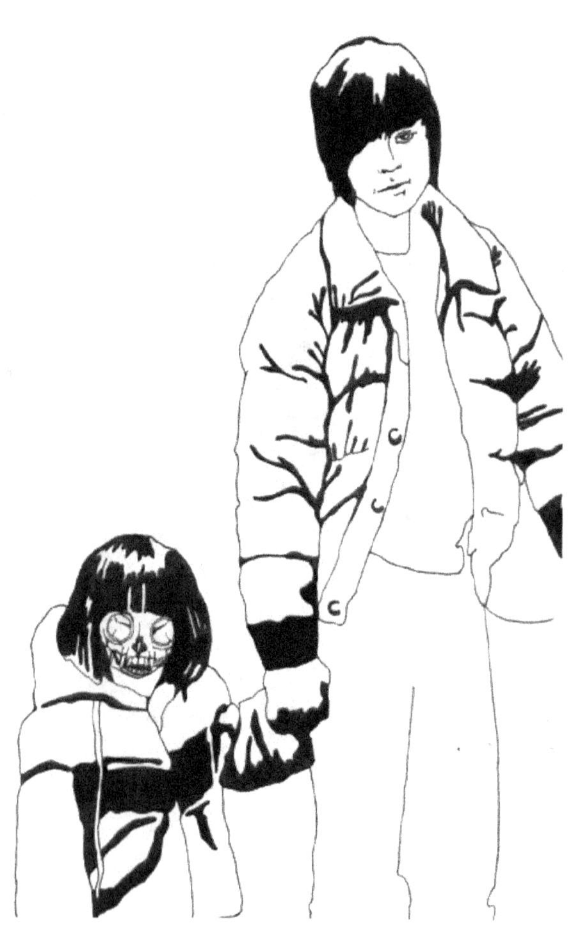

Unidentified

Rachel Pascua
from the family pictures series

Bloom Where You Are!

It was only the first week in March. The last batch of snow had barely melted. But the weather had taken an unusual turn, and before anyone knew it, it was 70 degrees out.

And this was all the encouragement that the rainbow of lawn crocuses had needed. Up they shot to let the world know that they had survived the winter and were ready to welcome spring, even if it wouldn't officially arrive for another 15 days.

These crocuses were not on one of the well-manicured lawns on the block. Those homeowners had carefully prepared their yards for winter.

The crocuses that I saw on this early morning in March had pushed their way up through un-raked leaves, rotting logs and decaying trash. If it's not my imagination, and crocuses really do tend to show up where they are most needed, this yard definitely needed their help.

Gold, purple and violet, white and yellow blossoms had simply nudged the trash and debris over just enough to make room for their slender leaves and pastel colors. This was where their roots were, so this was where these harbingers of spring would share their beauty.

It certainly wasn't the easiest place for them to grow. It would be nice if they could live in better surroundings. It would be nice if their contributions were welcomed with more open arms, in a yard that showed signs of appreciation.

Crocuses, however, simply
bloom where they are!

And if they're helpless to change their world, they're happy to make it a little brighter.

-B.F. Barcio, L.H.D.

Nothing to Say

The real-life account of a normal-ish person in a world full of judgmental nincompoops
By Madeline Daniel who likes long words.

I have nothing to say today. My work was tragically lost and I'm bored. I already promised I'd write something so I can't back out now.

Well anyway, I watched the original Superman movie the other night. It had a good premise, but how do they not recognize him as Clark Kent? So if I were to put on a pair of glasses and change my name, no one would recognize me?

I saw the weirdest thing the other day. I saw a lady carrying a monkey in a tutu in a cage. I swear I really saw it. If you don't believe me, ask anyone who was at the 2012 AAU National Karate Championships. This guy who knew told us it was a service monkey for the woman's anxiety. I had an anxiety attack the other night. Why don't I get a monkey to dress up? If I did, I'd dress it up like Superman.

I tried to be a vegetarian for a little while. But last night, we made homemade chicken nuggets and I just had to try one. I'm too weak to be a veggie.

-Madeline Daniel

A Powerless Point Lost Somewhere in the Middle

They call me Jishy, and they say the spirit of New York is in my father. He is a Bronx-born East Coast Jew who fled to Bloomington, Indiana for his Bachelor's and then law school, and later settled down in the "Midwestern metropolis" of Indianapolis, Indiana. He started practicing law, had one marriage and that one failed, and then he met my mother. They married and had two kids, and he still resides in Indianapolis to this day.

Every family member of my father's fled New York for California before I was born. So all I know of New York is from spending time with my father and his side of the family and from the New York Yankees. Los Angeles and New York are very far away from each other, but I grew up in Indianapolis... a powerless point lost somewhere in the middle.

I grew up visiting Los Angeles, my grandparents Nana and Baba. My Aunt Judi and Uncle Albert, Culver City, and the boardwalk of Seal Beach. It was a glorious time, teeming with sunshine and thick, New York style Judaism. It was more about the culture, and not so much the religion.

I had my boogie board and Baba's tomatoes. Cheese pizza by the slice and ice cream on the corner. Young Californian women with strong round asses flossed by thong bikini bottoms bouncing down the sand. And Dodger's games, golden, shimmering Dodgers in crisp white uni's with true blue trim, dancing on the green grass and sliding on the red clay diamond. The seats lining the stadium were yellowed like the pages of an old dictionary, sitting blissfully in the ravine. Oh those glorious nights of baseball, the night caps of beautiful, sun-soaked days at the beach, and the long, never ending traffic jams on the expressway. I can still feel it all like the scrape of sand caught between my skin and the elastic waistband of my swimsuit.

Those traffic jams have never ended, stuck in the back of my grandfather's Buick with my little brother and parents, impatient as only a young kid can be, but now there's no where else I'd choose. I'd bring Baba back to life with his rough whiskers and 3-4 bellybuttons. The extra holes were bullet wounds that he'd gotten defending his bar back in New York, years before I came into this world. Nana would be waiting back home for us to return from the beach. The crisp wind of an L.A. evening in the late 1980's.

The tomato garden. The green Astroturf on the front porch that led to the utility closet at the back. The one that held my boogie board safely, and protected it for the next time I would get to escape the Midwest, and get to spend time with New York in Los Angeles.

-Joshua Baratz

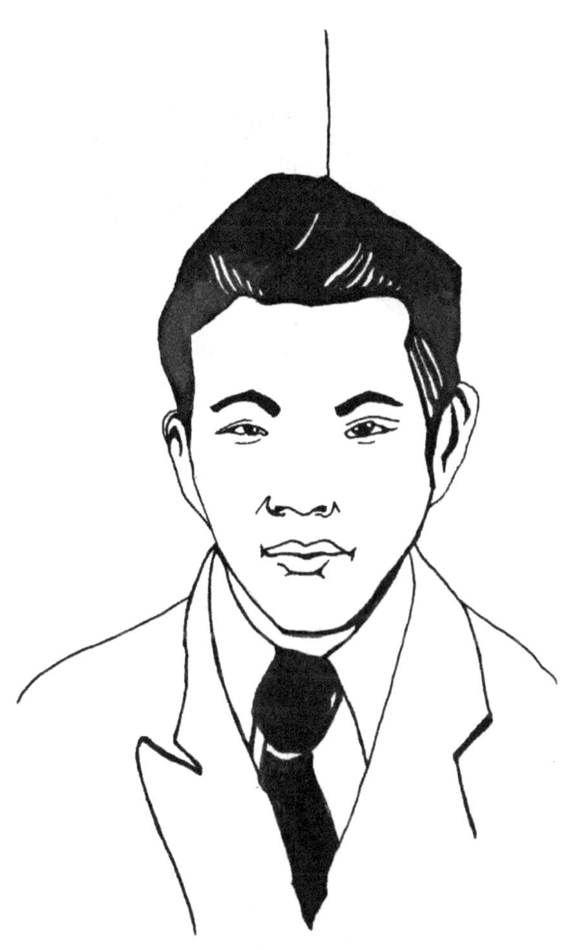

Lew York Hing

Rachel Pascua
from the lost series--executed murderers

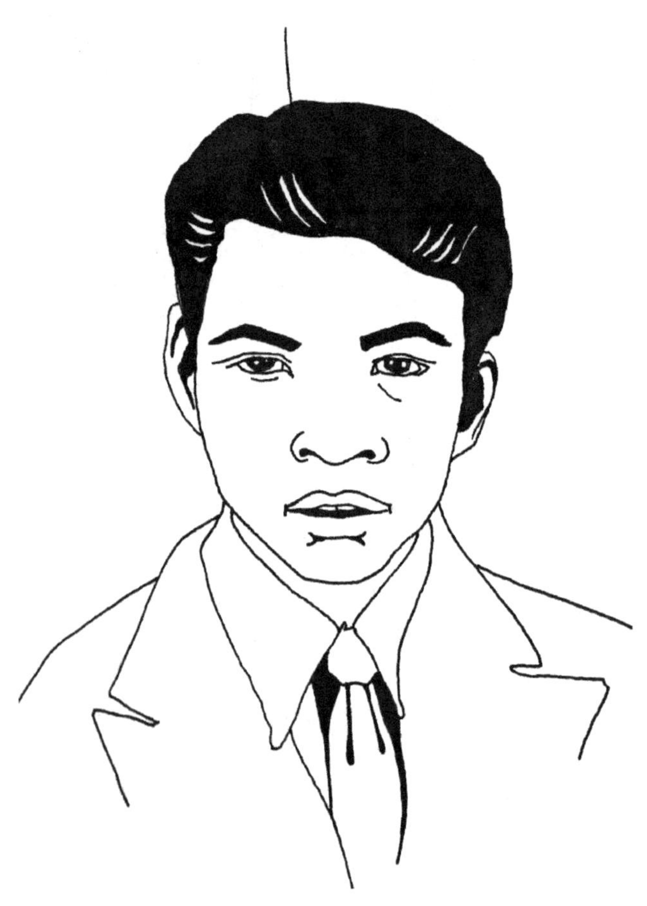

Yun Tieh Li

Rachel Pascua
from the lost series--executed murderers

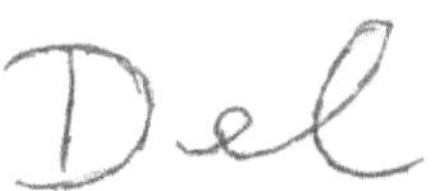

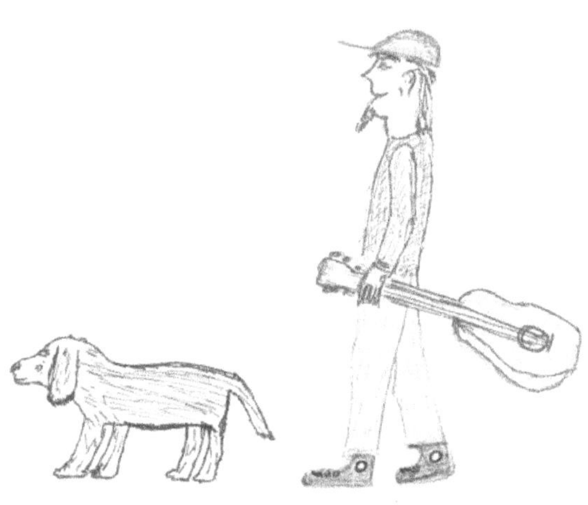

I had just finished a gig in Utah and was on my way to Winnemucca. I stopped in Baker to get some gas. Pulled out a map and realized I was going in the wrong direction. The attendant asked where I was headed. I said Los Angeles. A bit untruthful but I didn't want him to know I was lost. He noticed my guitar in the back seat and asked if I was a guitar player. I said I was just that. Also an inventor. He said there was a bar down the road that could always use some live entertainment. I told him I was no Johnny Cash but I'd been around. He didn't know who Johnny Cash was. That's OK I guess. I didn't know who Lola Falana was till recently. I headed to the bar. Nice name. "Stumble on Inn." I guess you're supposed to be drunk before you get there. So I stumbled on in and asked for the manager. Said I was passing through and the guy at the gas station said you might be looking for some live entertainment. He said that was his cousin Finn. He said being a weekday he could only give me $17.00 for the night. I said that's fine. After my fifth song the manager asked me if I was going to play the same song all night. I said: yes. He said: why? I said: that's the only song I know. (Folsom Prison Blues in F.) He said: get out. I said: fine. I said: what about my money? He said he had expected live entertainment to draw people in not chase them off. So I settled for a bag of pretzels. I stopped in to see Finn on the way out. He didn't remember me.

I headed for Tonopah. I heard the local grade school was looking for a guitar player to entertain the kid's on music day. Well I was playing my song and a kid in the back row was acting suspicious. My suspicions were confirmed when he reached in his lunch box a hurled an egg at me. He missed me but got my guitar on the fifth fret. Needless to say I came unglued. I was on him before he saw me coming. I worked over the little snot pretty good. Actually he wasn't that little. He was kind of big for a second grader. While being escorted off the school grounds the Principal said the only reason I wasn't being arrested was because nobody liked the kid anyway. On the way out of town I noticed a Calypso contest was being held next to the gas station. First prize was two weeks supply of "Harry Belafonte's Gourmet Prune Juice." I came in second. No prize for second place.

Pulled into Sandy Valley this morning. I've been living in a trailer behind the burned down gunnysack factory. Picked up my mail and there was a letter from Hilda. Hilda works at the Acme Guitar Factory and was trying to get them to consider one of my inventions. It's a combination guitar and rifle case.

I went to town. My stock of prune paste was running low. I couldn't find it so I asked the manager. He said: What the hell is prune paste? I said: Me thinks' it's just crushed prunes with a little corn meal added for texture. I told him I had just recently bought some off a road vendor. He said: don't you think it's a little dangerous buying homemade food from stranger? I said: I buy reconstituted corn dogs all the time off a guy who sells them out of his trunk. He just stared then asked me to leave.

I picked up the Sandy Valley paper today. There was a big shake up at Acme. Seems Hilda was an escaped mental patient. She was being taken back to the facility. They stopped at a Taco Bell for lunch. Hilda asked to use the restroom. The Federal Marshal checked things out and gave the okay. Five minutes later the Marshal sent the waitress in. Hilda was gone. The investigators say someone had hidden a Martina Navratilova costume in the restroom. Seems the costume shop down the street had sold that very costume earlier in the day. Hilda must have had an accomplice. Authorities aren't worried. This being an election year they believe Hilda will probably resurface as a candidate for the U.S. Senate.

I did some picking in front of Taco Bell this morning. The manager said I could play if I was 200 feet from the entrance. I played for about a half hour till the Police ran me off. I did stop by the K-Mart outlet. I was looking for some green high top converse tennis shoes. Mine were pretty worn. They're becoming kind of a trademark. Guess what happens next? I get home and there's an eviction notice telling me I have one week to get out. I checked with the Sheriff's office. The guy who rented it to me had been using it as a meth lab. I don't know what that is. All I know is it's now evidence and I'll be moving. I'd heard some good things about Amargosa Valley.

On my way to Amargosa Valley I stopped by Maybelle's place. She was gone! There was a big plywood sign where the trailer had been. All it said was "Kiss my ass." That Maybelle. What a card. We were married once for a couple minutes. After the ceremony she was seen talking to a guy in a purple cape. She ran off screaming. Wouldn't let me on her property after that.

I stopped in Indian Springs. Saw a guy selling used pencils in front of the café. He said his name was David White Eagle. Sounded familiar. Said his dad was Charlie White Eagle. Bingo! Me and Charlie were best pals. We even shared a refrigerator box behind the old icehouse in Vegas. David said his dad was killed a few years back. He was trying to grab a speeding pickup and was hit by another a car. I miss Charlie.

Arrived in Amargosa Valley. Set myself

up at the Post Office and started looking around for a place to stay. I smelled it before I saw it. Yes, a pig farm. The owner Maynard was out feeding the pigs. I told him I was looking for a place to stay. He said he had a trailer out back I could have for free. All I had to do was keep an eye on the pigs when he wasn't around. I told him I was raised on a pig farm. The deal was struck. The trailer was a big one. I'm guessing about 200 square feet. I'll get used to the extra space. Later Maynard brought over a couple Grape Nehis. We watched the sun go down. We both agreed it didn't get any better than this.

Maynard brought me the paper. The local band was looking for a lead guitarist. I showed up and you should have seen the expression on their faces when they saw me. Word must have got out that I was in town. When they saw the tennis shoes they must have put two and two together. They wanted to know my background. I told them I didn't have one. I was raised on a pig farm. When oil was discovered on the farm Pa offered me $300.00 a month if I would get out and never come back. An offer I couldn't refuse. I picked up a guitar at a swap meet and the rest is history. They said: shall we try something? Sure I said.

How about Folsom Prison Blues in F? So I started to play. About five seconds into the song they stopped. I said: what's wrong? The rhythm guy said: I thought you said F? I said: I was in F. He asked if my guitar was tuned. I said: yes, by a guitar shop in Mexico. He said there was a good chance the guy who tuned it didn't know what he was doing. I said: I beg to differ. He said: what's the deal with the fifth fret? I said it was damaged by a flying egg and was also repaired in Mexico. He said: the fact that the fret sticks out farther than the rest explains the dead sound. I told him I hadn't had any complaints. He said: what kind of an idiot plays a guitar in this condition? I said: I wouldn't know. He said he saw a guitar once like that in Toys "R" Us. He also said the strings were on backward. I told him if he knew so much about guitars what was he doing in Amargosa Valley? That got him. I left.

We'll yesterday didn't go too good. The thing about the strings being on backwards kind of bugged me. I stopped in Guitars "R" Us and looked at some models. Sure enough the strings were on just the opposite of mine. I asked the salesman if perchance his guitars were strung wrong. He stared at me for a good twenty seconds. I've seen that stare before. Then he said they were strung for people who play standing on their head. It all made sense now.

Maynard invited me over to the big house. He whipped up a pitcher of mesquite tea. Then we went into town for some supplies. You're not going to guess what comes next. Getting off the bus was none other than Hilda. She had tracked me down from an old letter I had written when she worked at Acme. We all drove back to the farm. Hilda was impressed with everything she saw. I knew what she was thinking. Little Del's running around. You guessed it. Wedding bells. Again I know what you're thinking. Who was Hilda's accomplice? Hilda says that's for another time. Right now I'm working on a new invention. It's a throw away guitar.

THROW AWAY GUITAR

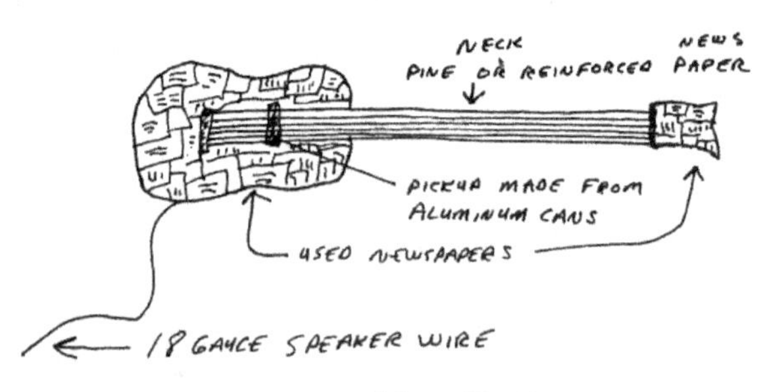

NOTE: NO TUNING NOBS NEEDED

Well we're just lying back on the farm. Hilda now has a new identity. Mrs. Hilda Krebs. Not much chance of them catching her now. Maynard ran an extension cord out to the trailer, so we now have electricity. I've been working pretty hard on the throw away guitar. I think I'm going to take the blueprints up to Acme in person. Just a side note: Me and Hilda have been practicing Wildwood Flower in our spare time. Looks like we have a duet brewing.

Hilda has decided to stay home while I head up to Acme. I'm kind of worried, about the protesters in front of the farm. But Maynard will be there. I'll be on the road for a couple days.

Time on the road was shorter than I expected. Stayed overnight at a rest stop. I know what you're thinking. Yes I did. I set up by the restroom and played until a Forest Ranger told me to stop bothering people.

Pulled into Acme before they opened, so I sat under a tree by the front door and did a little picking. One guy gave me a dollar. I told the secretary I was an inventor and would like to talk to someone about a new guitar design. Four hours later I was escorted in to somebody's office. He introduced himself. There was that look again. I told him I had invented a throw away guitar. He noticed my blueprints were written on a napkin. He kept staring so I broke the ice. I told him I was also a guitar player and from experience had noticed that a lot of time was spent on carrying a guitar around not to mention maintenance. I told him if the guitar was a throw away those problems would be eliminated. The guitar could be bought at WalMart before the gig and after the gig thrown in the trash. It would be made of newspapers that the employees could bring from home. It would be pre-tuned, so no need for tuning knobs. The body strength would come from gluing the papers together. Elmer's glue should work fine. The pickups are made out of recycled aluminum cans. The guitar strings would be manufactured by a good friend of mine who has a music store in Mexicali. The cord would be 18 gauge speaker wire, built into the guitar. The other end would have a plug for the amp of course. He didn't talk, just stared. Then finally he asked how I expected the neck to hold up under the string tension? I said the neck could be made one of two ways. It could be made out of pine, or made out of paper with a steel rod inside for strength. He said: what if it gets out of tune during the session? I said:

the tuning is guaranteed to last for two hours. About that time two security guards who had been hanging around showed up and escorted me to my car.

I wasn't discouraged though. I've been through this many times. I headed back home. I drove straight through, arriving in Amargosa Valley a little before dark. You'll never guess what I saw. Actually I heard it first. Hilda and Maynard were jamming to Wildwood Flower. Maynard really made that French horn sing. That Maynard. What a sneak. A pig farmer and a musician! We played a little, and then sat down for some mesquite tea. Hilda walked off to chase the pigs. I know what you're thinking. Me and Maynard were thinking it too. Forming a band. We thought of a name. Since I was already famous around these parts, we thought we'd call it "The Del Krebs Trio."

Got up real early, being excited about our new idea. Went to town for a paper. They're having a talent contest in Winnemucca at the local feed store. Talked with Hilda and Maynard about maybe going up. The only problem might be the pigs. Who would feed them while we were gone? Guess what? Problem solved. We'd take them with us. I know what you're thinking. How do we transport that many pigs? Did I forget to mention, the farm only has three pigs? Arnold the house pig uses the doggy door, no problem, so he will stay to guard the house. Maynard has a small trailer that U-Haul gave to him saying it wasn't road worthy. Looks like The Del Krebs Trio and two pigs are on their way to Winnemucca.

Maynard's saying we have to get the trailer licensed, so we went down to the DMV. We had the trailer tied pretty securely with chain around the bumper. The guy doing the inspecting asked if this was a joke. I told him I was a guitar player and inventor, not a comedian. He asked what we were hauling? I said pigs. He said: you can't haul livestock in a trailer tied to the bumper, with no trailer hitch. He also said: what kind of crazy person actually does something like this? I told him Maynard wasn't crazy. He just stared at me. It's a good thing Maynard wasn't close by at the time. He used to be a security guard at WalMart and there's no telling what would have happened. To make a long story short, we didn't get the license. We weren't discouraged though. Maynard said: let's make like horseshit and hit the trail. That's what we did.

Back home Hilda was whipping up

some fried baloney sandwiches and we invited Maynard over for dinner. We were thinking what to do when a light went off in my head. We could leave the pigs here and I know just the guy to watch them. David White Eagle. I would drive to Indian Springs tomorrow and see if he was still around.

David was right where I left him. He said just give him an address and he'd be there but we were leaving in the morning, so David drove back with me. He said not to make any fuss; he'd sleep with the pigs. He said the grunting was kind of soothing.

Well were leaving. We're going to try to drive straight through. I told David we'd be back in a couple days. Stopped by WalMart for a case of oil. The old Rambler does burn a little oil. A case should be enough. We also picked up some green high tops for Hilda and Maynard. We don't want to look like a bunch of Hicks. Had a hard time fitting Hilda. Twelve was the biggest size. Hilda said no problem; she'd just cut out the toes.

We stopped in Austin at the "Harry Reid Café." We ate lunch, and I bought a ten-page book about Harry's lifetime accomplishments. We stopped at a swap meet on the way out. Picked up some matching t-shirts for the contest. Hilda bought some corn nuts. The shirts had a picture of Ed Roman the famous guitar builder on the front. Hilda kind of admired Ed. She say's he sang the greatest version of Wildwood Flower she ever heard.

We pulled into Winnemucca and went directly to the feed store to sign up. First prize was a six months supply of Castile soap. It wasn't so much the prize, although that was really something to shoot for. The main thing is that winning would open the door to a recording contract.

We checked in a Motel. There was nothing to do till tomorrow so we talked over what we were going to play. You guessed it. Wildwood Flower with Folsom Prison Blues as a backup in case we were asked to do another. We practiced a little till the manager made us quit. We didn't need any practice anyway.

We were scheduled to perform second. The contest was in the barn that stored all the feed. The announcer had to leave once in a while to help customers. There were two judges, and a crowd of about ten people.

The first contestant had finished. The crowd sure seemed excited. I guess they never saw anyone play the harmonica and yodel at the same time before.

Well we were up. Hilda started to sing and it looked like we were going to nail this thing, when all of a sudden a cow pie hit Hilda on the shoulder. I could see her expression change from one of just having a good time to madness. She continued singing though, being a professional. When the next pie hit all hell broke loose. Hilda lifts weights and is 250 pounds of solid muscle. I knew what was coming. Hilda was on top of the pie thrower before anybody realized what was happening. We got there before Hilda could do too much damage. Me and Maynard and two other guys finally got her off the guy. Everybody else had left by then. When Hilda screams it's best to get out. The guy was out cold but still breathing. We figured it was best to get out of there, Hilda being on the lam and all. I asked the one judge who was still there who he thought the winner was? He said he couldn't make that call but the manager had told him to give us the soap if we'd get Hilda off the premises. I asked him if he thought maybe there was a talent scout in the audience. He just stared. I took that as a no. We left.

We got Hilda calmed down back at the motel. It took a six-pack of coke and 12 bags of corn nuts but we did it.

On the way back home we started wondering if the guy Hilda pounded was maybe a plant in the audience. We think maybe they wanted the yodeler to win. The cow pies had to be brought in from the outside, there weren't any cows walking around and the pies still retained some freshness.

We got home about sundown. We all gathered on the patio. The best time of day. We watched the sun drop through the smog behind what looked liked mountains. David White Eagle made a proposition. He asked if he could stay on. He'd still sell pencils in town, although the used pencil business was beginning to suck. Maynard was glad to have him on board. David had an idea that he believed might revive the pencil trade. He was thinking; why not have the pencils sharpened at both ends? I know what you're thinking: what about the eraser? You must have forgotten I'm an inventor. The eraser would be in the middle. Some small details to work out but this could revolutionize the pencil trade.

Maynard was thinking that maybe it would be better if we play in the same key when were playing. Most other bands play that way. He was thinking it might help

Hilda out too. David also said there had been a car parked out front yesterday. It appeared they were looking for someone. Alarm bells went off. Had they caught up to Hilda? We thought it best for Hilda to stay in the big house tonight and we'd figure this thing out in the morning.

I went to town in the morning. Figured I'd snoop around and find out who was casing our place. There was a stranger in town! I went into the diner to ask around and I thought I was seeing double. Hilda. But it wasn't Hilda. We struck up a conversation. You're not going to believe what comes next. Are you ready for this? She was Hilda's twin sister. She was looking for Hilda! I'm not through. Greta and Hilda had inherited a fortune from a rich Uncle. She was here to tell Hilda. Get this. Greta was the mysterious stranger who planted the Martina Navratilova costume. The plot thickens. Seems Hilda had been caught years ago trying to break in to the Acme Corn Nut factory. She was finishing up her time in the facility when her father decided it was best to leave her in there. That's when Greta took action. Hilda hid in the garbage and Greta drove the dump truck. The rest is history.

Greta had also got the charges

dropped.

Greta followed me home, and the minute they saw each other you should have heard Hilda scream. But this was a happy scream, not the kind we heard in Winnemucca. We don't have any furniture so we went over to the big house. Maynard was the perfect host. He served mesquite tea and bacon. Greta said her flight left in the morning and for us to decide what we wanted to do. In the morning Greta and Hilda went into town to set up a bank account. Greta left shortly after.

Looks like we're rich. First order of business is to get a complete tune-up on the Rambler. Hilda's thinking about a new straw hat and maybe some more weights. Meantime I've got lots of work to do on my new invention. Are you thinking it has something to do with a guitar? You're right. It's a guitar that converts into a coffee table. I know what you're thinking. Doesn't make sense. You'd be wrong. Makes perfect sense. Suppose me and Maynard are practicing.

Hilda says: coffees on!

A problem arises. No place to set the coffee.

Need I say more?

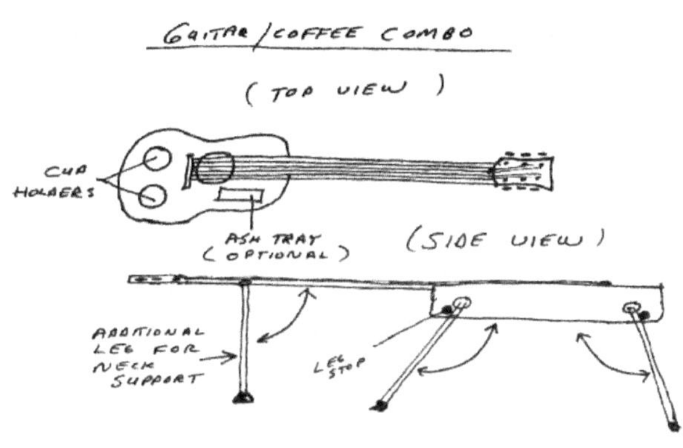

NOTE: ① WHEN IN PLAYING POSITION, LEGS ARE ATTACHED TO SIDE OF GUITAR WITH VELCRO
② RUBBER LEG TIPS SUPPLIED AT NO ADDITIONAL COST

Del here. Some interesting things to report. I've put the Kibosh on the guitar coffee table combo. You're wondering why? I'll explain. Suppose we're having our coffee and I get to thinking about a new note to add to my guitar solo. I reach for my guitar and knock all the coffee on the floor. I know what you're thinking. Why not get a spare guitar for situations like this? That's a possibility, but get this. I mention this problem to Maynard and guess what he says? He says: why not just buy a coffee table, WalMart has some nice ones? Again

Maynard comes out of nowhere with a solution. But just in case the blueprints will remain on file.

I see another problem arising. We were living pretty good on my monthly check and now with Hilda's inheritance thing are getting complicated. We went down to the bank. Me and Hilda that is. We were talking to the Manager about what we should do when we needed money. He said we could go to an ATM machine with this card he showed us, stick it in and get money out. I didn't like that idea. I didn't like it one bit. He said there's another way. We could write a check when we buy something and the money would come out of the account. I inquired what a check was. He explained. I said: so you're telling me I have to carry around these checks all the time, not to mention a pen? He said: checks are little and would fit in my pocket. I didn't like this idea either. He said Hilda could also carry them in her purse. I said: Hilda doesn't own a purse. Meanwhile I notice Hilda's hand. She's starting to form a fist. Bad sign. I knew we only had a minute to get out of there. The manager says: Millionaires usually conduct business in the manner I have described, but you can also just come in and just get the cash. I say: Now we were getting somewhere. So if the need arises, that's what we're going to do. I cashed my monthly check before we left. We stopped in the used clothing store for a straw hat Hilda had her eyes on, then back home. I was working with David on the new pencil design.

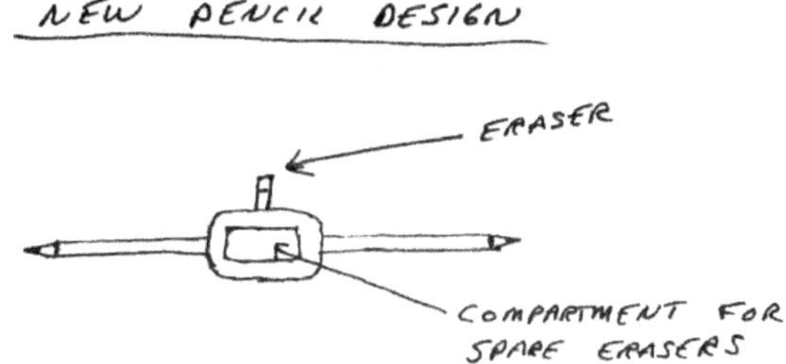

NOTE : PENCILS AND ERASER UNSCREW FOR EASY STORAGE

You were probably wondering why I was so eager to leave home in the first place. Well I was kind of a free spirit and Pop didn't like that.

An example: One day they had some company over. Me and Boomer were headed outside to play catch. Boomer stopped and took a crap on the coffee table. You would have thought it was the end of the world. It's not like Boomer hadn't done this before. I'm thinking: big deal, Mom's thinking disaster. This is just one example of many.

Enough about me. A couple days ago when I was picking up aluminum cans by the dump, I spotted a pile of wood. Probably from a construction site. I asked Maynard if I could borrow his pickup. Maynard said he'd go with me and help. He asked what I had up my sleeve. I said I couldn't let this opportunity pass. Looked like enough wood to build some furniture with. Nothing fancy. Maybe a kitchen table first and then (you guessed it) a coffee table.

You're probably wondering what happened to Boomer. He went under shortly after the crapping incident. Just old age. I had a private funeral. Just me and my cousin Virgil were in attendance. The burial was in a private place. Only me and Virgil know the location. I miss old Boomer.

I was taking a break from building the furniture. Me and Hilda decided to go for a little drive. We headed out Route 373 past the Old Farm Road. We saw a help wanted sign in the window of "Amargosa Feed and Tack." We stopped in. They were looking for someone to stack the bales of hay. The guy said the bales weighed between 75 and 125 pounds. He said it looked like I didn't even weigh that much. Hilda said: what about me? The guy kind of snickered. Well to make a long story short, Hilda walked outside, grabbed one bale in each hand and dropped them in front of the guy. Looks like Hilda has a job. It's only part time though. Just when the hay is delivered.

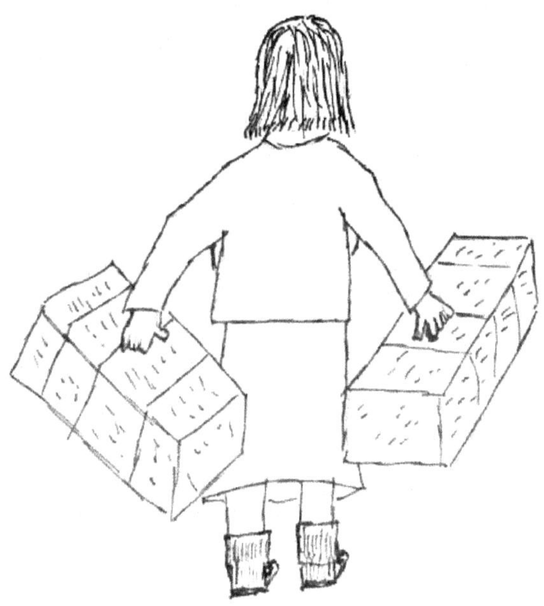

The Rambler's been acting up lately, so we stopped in an auto repair place Maynard recommended. The guy said the engine wasn't going to last much longer, and a lot of the other parts were about to fall off. I said: How much? He said: Doesn't matter, the parts aren't available for this car any more. I said: How can this be? It's only 40 years old. He said: This might be the only Rambler still on the road. I said: so it's probably worth a lot of money? He just stared. We left.

On the way home Hilda says maybe we could buy a new car. I said: It's up to you Baby Cakes. Hilda said: Wouldn't hurt to look. I agreed. Me and Hilda always agree.

We left early the next day to do some car shopping. We pulled into a car place and started nosing around. I told the guy (who was there in 2 seconds) we were thinking about maybe a pickup. He asked how much I was looking to spend. I said that was up to the Missus. The one he showed us had extra seats in the back, just like a car. This made sense seeing as how we usually took Maynard or David with us, not to mention the musical instruments. He said: This particular model is $35,000.00. I asked Hilda what she thought. She said: It's up to you Baby Cakes. Yes we call each other Baby Cakes.

We made the deal and drove into town to get the money. A couple hours later we were driving a new pickup. Hilda was actually. I drove the Rambler home.

Well we pulled up to the trailer. Maynard was in the yard with David. You should have seen their faces. You might be wondering about the Rambler. We're keeping it for a spare.

Maynard's hand was all bandaged up. I asked what happened. He said he'd been showing David how to drive and they drove into a ditch. Maynard said the truck was totaled. He wasn't sure what he was going to do. A pickup was pretty essential in farm work. He was pretty upset.

Me and Hilda stepped off to the side to discuss Maynard's situation. Seeing as how Maynard was our best friend we decided to give him the new pickup. Of course when we gave the keys to Maynard, he thought it was a joke or something. I said: no joke, just one drawback. When the Rambler is out of service, he might have to give us a ride to town or maybe take Hilda to work. He couldn't talk. I took that as a yes.

Got a letter back from the Acme Pencil Company. They thanked me for my interest in promoting the pencil trade. They said the blueprints had been submitted to their engineering department and they had rejected them. Reason being that the pencil weighed close to a pound and the results of testing showed that writing time had to be limited to 20 minutes.

You might think I'd be discouraged by this letter. You'd be wrong. I have another idea. I'm thinking this pencil might be just the thing for Scuba Divers. They could carry it to the bottom with them. It would be there in case they needed to write something down and would also serve as a weight. Only problem being that it probably wouldn't write underwater. I'll work on that.

I told David the news. He said: no problemo. (He'd learned that from a Mexican.) He said he was staying as far away from pencils as he could for the time being. He also said that Maynard had made him foreman of the farm.

A load of hay had come in and Hilda had to work. I dropped her off and me and Maynard thought we'd play a little. Maynard suggested that instead of taking the Trio on the road why didn't we make a recording and send it in to the recording studio. Maynard said he had an old cassette recorder in the shed and we could get blank cassettes at WalMart.

We drove into town in Maynard's new truck. I had to stop at the bank. I withdrew $20.00. I wasn't sure how much a cassette tape would cost.

We got home but didn't dare start without Hilda. We picked up Hilda, stopped for some corn nuts and headed home to do some recording. Hilda whipped up some fried baloney sandwiches. We went over to the big house to practice. Maynard had chairs in case we wanted to sit down.

David would work the recorder. We decided on a duet with me and Hilda. Maynard said he didn't sing on a professional level like we did and he would just concentrate on the rhythm. We sang "Just between the two of us." It looked like we nailed it on the first cut, but when David said he forgot to put in a cassette we made another one. David played it back. There was a lot of static, but we thought the recording company wouldn't mind. They probably had equipment to take the static out.

So the recording session lasted around 15 minutes. We were ready to put it in the mail. We just had to pick a recording company. We picked Acme.

The kitchen table's done. Might get a splinter though if you're not careful. Now to get some chairs. We decided on four.

We had to go into town to mail the

recording so we all jumped in Maynard's truck. We stopped in WalMart to look at furniture. We saw the chairs we liked in the furniture department. Looked like quality. The fact that they folded up was a plus. Nothing left but a sofa and the trailer will be pretty well furnished.

Hilda likes her job. She says it keeps her in shape. I'm still going to surprise her with a new set of weights for her birthday though.

Were sticking close to home. I have to be ready to leave on a minutes' notice when the recording company writes back. I'm working on a new invention. It's a guitar that folds up. It will easily fit inside a small suitcase. I'm having a surprise birthday party for Hilda. Greta is flying in. Probably staying at some big hotel in Vegas. I've only been in Vegas once, that time with Charlie White Eagle.

By the way, I know what you're thinking. What about the money, being rich and all that? I'm sure Greta will have something to say about that too. Actually neither me nor Baby Cakes cares for money that much. If we have a need someday, we know where it is.

-Frank Morelli

UFOs, Cigarettes, Elephant Collectibles

Mr. Fishburn called me to list one of his rental properties over on Dawson Street. He told me he's sick of "those people." He said, "They're dis-GUST-ing!"

An accurate, un-biased description of the daily routine of the tenants in question is as follows: They wake up, they smoke, they eat, they switch on the TV, they smoke, they watch TV, they talk about what's on TV, they go to the bathroom, they talk about what happened in the bathroom, they smoke, they go to sleep.

Fishburn is Irish Catholic, the oldest of twelve kids and gay. His father told him he can't forgive him, not because he's gay but because he's a slumlord. Fishburn owns scores of rental houses on the east side and rents exclusively to poor people.

Ask Fishburn about the Irish and he'll tell you, "They're dis-GUS-ting!"

Catholics?

"Dis-GUS-ting!"

Hillbillies?

"Dis-GUS-ting!"

Gays?

"Dis-GUS-ting!"

He makes fun of me for being

descended from Italians. He says, "You smell like garlic! You like that Eye-talian sausage? You can come over to my house and eat sausage!"

I tell Mr. Fishburn, "Go watch a DVD about the history of planet Earth then come and talk to me about who's disgusting."

Who's in charge of this place? The end could come at any moment. People's opinions of each other don't matter.

I agreed to take the listing on Dawson Street only if Fishburn sprang for Otis. Otis is expensive, but he can make any dump look like a palace. He moves everything around, lights it up nice. Otis' photographs move houses.

Fishburn agreed. He's hateful, not stupid.

I told Otis to meet me at 1138 Dawson Street at eleven thirty-eight in the morning. I was being cute. I told him not to leave anything expensive in the car. And not to bring his expensive car. I told him to bring whatever he has in his arsenal to do magic.

UFOs

1138 Dawson Street. One-level Victorian with a partially finished attic. Is that one-story or two stories? Full basement.

Full of garbage. Full of water.

I parked on the street fifteen minutes early. A rare occurrence for me. Earliness is next to impossibleness.

I sat in the car waiting for Otis. The drizzle on the windshield made all the houses and the trees look even sadder than I knew they were. Sitting in the car made my stomach hurt. I got out and felt the trickle of raindrops on my shaved head. It felt wrong. It's the coal plant down the road. It rains here and the siding on the houses gets dirtier.

I walked up and took shelter beneath the historic charmer's gabled porch roof, admiring its gingerbread woodwork and decorative touches. I ran my hand over the cracking support columns and approached the dusty-but-ornate stained glass, original front door. I heard the sound of television coming from within. I put my ear up to the door and listened.

I heard the word Roswell. They were watching a show about UFOs.

I imagined him on the couch, her on the recliner. Television in the corner. Cigarette smoke permeating everything. The conspiracy being laid out in detail before their eyes.

The cover-up. Smoke and mirrors.

Exactly what I had come there to do. I wanted to yell through the door, "I'm in on it!"

A red Audi pulled up. It was Otis, the photographer. He parked behind my Jetta.

Two shirtless kids leaned out the side door of an aluminum-sided duplex across the street. A bewildered teenaged woman appeared behind them and glared at us. I waved to them. The woman shooed the boys inside and closed the door.

She was protecting them from the future. Audi and a Jetta. Realtor and a photographer. There goes the neighborhood.

Otis popped his trunk and pulled out an array of lights and reflector boards. He hoisted his equipment up on his shoulder, clicked the remote lock on the Audi and met me at the porch stairs.

I held my hands up like a display model. "What do you think?"

Otis nodded. "Great woodwork. Terrific porch. The outside is beautiful."

I smiled. The outside is beautiful. I have heard that said about a lot of things. Houses. People. Coffins.

"Is someone living here?" Otis asked.

"Renters. I told them we wouldn't be too disruptive."

Otis raised an eyebrow.

I knocked on the door. I heard a loud thump, then pitter-patter. The door swung open and we were greeted by a human being known to me to be dis-GUS-ting in the opinion of her landlord. Approximately forty-five years old, upwards of three hundred and fifty pounds, stringy, dishwater-blonde hair, pink sweat pants, white socks and a knee-length t-shirt adorned with a faded, airbrushed facsimile of the Tasmanian Devil.

She exhaled smoke and smiled. "When you say eleven thirty-eight, you mean it!"

"Every once in a while I do."

Behind her on the TV was a grainy black and white image of an alien on an examination table. She caught me looking at it.

"Wild, ain't it? Well, don't just stand there." She stood aside and yelled to someone I could not yet see. "Get up! Photographer's here!"

I waved. "Don't get up. It's okay. We can work around you."

CIGARETTES

She held a lit cigarette in one hand and the rest of the pack in her other hand. This is something I have observed my mother-in-law and her sisters do. They take their pack of cigarettes with them as they move throughout the house, even when they are already smoking one. Like a boyscout-ish level of ultra-preparedness. They don't carry their money or their keys or their identification as many places as they carry their cigarettes.

She plopped back down in her recliner and looked at Otis' collection of gadgets. "I've never seen anything like this before."

Otis smiled. "We'll try not to be too disruptive."

My eyes adjusted to the darkness and the haze. The man of the house coughed and I saw him on the couch. He wore a Harley Davidson t-shirt and tight blue running shorts that bulged immensely from the strain of his enormity. He was a massive, gentle presence in the room, and one I instantly had no fear of.

I know from experience that nobody's harmless. But that said, this man, this woman. They mean no harm.

The lady of the house threw her weight back in the chair, extending the recliner out to its full horizontal setting. "I've heard of taking pictures of the outside of the house like for the house books at the grocery."

"Whelp," Otis leaned his light stands against the wall, "this is just like that. But with the Internet, you know, people want to go see a house without going to see the house.

She exhaled a cloud of smoke and nodded. "Vir-tu-al re-al-ity."

I smiled. "It's a time saver."

"Times," the man on the couch blurted out, "are changing." He turned the volume up on the TV using the remote.

I wondered if they were brother and sister or man and wife. I made a mental note to be on the look out for clues.

The man smoked softly, gently, holding the smoke in for long periods of time. I had a sense of his smoking all the while we were there, but I never heard him exhale, or light one up, or crush one out. I heard the strained inhalation. But this man was an expert at being in the background. This was an accomplishment on his part, considering his size. Or it was surrender.

As we moved from room to room, Otis and I were always in it, the smoke, the haze, the fog.

We moved to the kitchen and cleared the counters of dirty dishes, newspapers and ashtrays. Clear counter space creates the illusion of a big kitchen.

There were two, open, half-used, crusted-over bottles of mustard on top of the refrigerator, an easy opportunity for judgment if one were looking for an excuse to judge. But let's face it. How many bottles of mustard do the rest of us have in our homes? I might have three for all I know. I buy one whenever I am planning for a cookout, because from the sterile sanctuary of the Safeway, surrounded by more products than I know what to do with, it just makes sense to me. "Buy mustard! You might not have any at home." So the inventory grows and the mustard industry has us all in it's slimy, yellow grip.

Otis snapped a few shots of the room with its newly cleared counters then we headed for the dining room. We passed under an arch, where above us hung a hand-carved wooden sign: *"So it ain't home sweet home. Adjust!"*

The television announcer said, "We will return to The Truth About Roswell."

The man of the house shouted that he did not believe the cars at the Indianapolis Motor Speedway would be able to qualify today an account of the rain, but that they might get some practice in because the rain was supposed to stop around one o'clock.

The woman coughed. "Where'd you

hear that?"

"The National Weather Service."

The way he enunciated made me respect that organization as an authority on the subject.

ELEPHANT COLLECTIBLES

On display in the dining room were many objects that in one way or another resembled an elephant. Elephant salt and pepper shakers, elephant coasters, teapot with elephant-ear handles and a trunk for a spout, an elephant's face hand-painted on the plump carafe.

Elephant inspirational poster, elephant calendar, pink plastic vase with three-dimensional moldings of elephants roaming around a Serengeti landscape. Three dried up, long-stem flowers stuck out of the vase.

Otis snapped a picture of the flowers and looked at me. "Never had a chance."

He set his camera down and set up his lights. I began moving things out of the scene, like we had done in the kitchen.

Otis stopped me. "You don't have to do that. Most of this is just going to disappear in the background."

Suddenly I saw everything in the room as me. This job, my life. It's all going to disappear into the background.

The narrator of the Roswell documentary took a turn for the historical, referencing a list of world events that occurred simultaneously to, or around the same time as the goings on at Area 51. Atom bomb tests. Suburban expansion. Micro-electronic advancements. Hearing history in that context made the UFO sightings seem so real. So intertwined with the culture.

I peeked in the living room and saw the lady of the house struggling to stand up from her recliner. She said, "I never even heard of Roswell till this show came on."

The man got up from the couch and walked over to give her a hand. "This occurred in 1947. 1947!"

"Well, I wasn't alive in 1947."

"You can't prove it."

"I got a birth certificate around here somewhere's'll prove it."

"Anybody kin fake a birth certificate."

She popped up out of the chair and into his arms. He giggled. She slapped him on the arm and pushed past him toward the bathroom.

They were married. I knew it now.

My father told me once, "You get married when you find the person you'd like to annoy for the rest of your life."

Maybe Mr. Fishburn will get lucky and the Indiana State Senate will decide to allow him and his partner the same bliss as Italians and Irish and Catholics and hillbillies are granted by our constitution. The right to annoy each other officially forever and to smoke and grow enormous and watch TV and talk about what's on TV. The right to life, man! Isn't that what everybody is arguing about?

Otis tapped me on the shoulder. "We're all done inside. I just need some exterior shots and a shot of the garage."

The man of the house stood humbly before us. "I hope it wud-n't too much'v a mess."

I smiled at him. "Have you found a new place yet?"

"No, we're just packin' things up, gettin' ready."

"You haven't found a place to move?"

"Nope, nope. Ain't even started looking."

Then why are you packing, I thought? Is that the best utilization of your time? Packing when you haven't found a place to move yet?

I handed him my card. "Give me a call. I might be able to help you out."

"Oh," he looked at the card. "Well, we don't have a phone we can use right now."

"Come by the office then," I said. "Or how `bout I'll stop by later and we can talk? It won't cost you anything."

"That'd be alright I guess."

I shook his hand. It was completely limp, like shaking hands with an enormous, Jell-o-filled stuffed animal. He gave Otis the same limp handshake then turned and opened the front door. The light from outside was blinding.

-Phillip Barcio

Boys will be Boys

The arcade was too crowded for Connor and Declan. A new mud, called Hane's Noon, created a stir in Web. The game required that your mem chips, eye gogs, gui-gloves, and earpieces be imbedded into your skull. No more peripheries, no more hard upgrades. And you had to be 13, an adult, to get the procedure, which to a 9 and 7 year old, was completely unfair.

Two boys in a gray street tube strode the slowest belt. No rush, since the ambient artificial light of the domed city hadn't begun to fade, signifying night. Declan suggested "follow the leader" on the faster, commuter belts. Connor yawned disapproval, and conversed with Web's local map, uploaded the 3d peg of a girl he saw at the arcade, and played a first person shooter game. All in his head. He'd already finished his diffy q homework.

Not wanting to go home, Dec decided to get into trouble. Not consciously, but when Declan saw an empty building and light encryption, he needed to see what was inside.

"We'll use your gogs, Dec," Connor commanded the operation, suddenly interested. Connor searched Web for the registration, got an owner's name, then a medrec. From the medrec, a retinal. He passed it on to Declan. Dec had rewired his perfs 100s of times, so 180ing the emitter was easy. Holding it up to the lock, click.

Inside was green grass, trees, and sunshine.

In the spring of 2880, a religious terrorist group attempted to alter the path of Asteroid 1950 DA, so that it would collide with Earth. Partially thwarted, debris from the explosions inside the asteroid pelted the Earth, killing millions and subjecting the planet to a decades long "nuclear" winter. 2 Billion lost their lives in total.

The people of Earth snapped. All religions, peaceful or otherwise, were banned. Churches and mosques razed. Priests, and monks, and imams, and nuns crucified. The Mob wanted a total destruction of all spiritual thought. The Materialists rose, riding the idea that man was only a machine, a complex set of biochemical reactions. DNA was the new God. Spiritualists and spirituality became swear words. There was no noticeable underground.

Technology had to be reinvented.

Cities needed to be domed, since the atmosphere never fully recovered. A one-world government rose, and soon absorbed all the new colonies of Man through out the Western Spiral Arm.

The government controlled the only source of information, now known as Web. Web ran the trains, grew the food, built cities, and created a completely cerebral existence for humans.

Jack, Connor and Declan's father, once worked for the gov't. He knew which parts of the above story were true, and which weren't.

That's why Jack quit his gov't job, and now writes software for asteroid mining robots. His wife, Barbara, helps assimilate those communities outside the Dome system, reintegrating those left behind back into this new, perfect society.

On disk, it was the perfect family.

"Do you hear that?"

"What?... I don't... hear... anything? Web, what is this flower I am looking at? Web, are you there?" Connor begins to panic. "I don't have any access?" He takes his earpiece out of his ear, something he hasn't done in over a year. The LED is not green. The LED is not any color.

"Where are we?" asks young Declan.

"You are in my Garden."

The children see a very old man. Or at least, he first appears to be old. His posture is perfect and his eyes sparkle, despite their almond shape.

"The flower you see is called Sakura, also known as a cherry blossom. You're very lucky. They just opened today and will be gone in two days."

"Gone. Where do they go?" Declan smiled.

"They fall to the ground and pass away, giving back to the Earth. They are both brief and beautiful."

Connor puts his arm around his little brother. "How do we leave?" he demands.

"Turn around and walk away. But, you're always welcome here."

Connor tries to turn Declan, but Dec's having none of it. "My name is Declan. What's yours?"

"Suke. I'm glad to meet you, Declan. And is this your brother?"

"His name is Conn..." Declan tries to say, but Connor puts his hand over the boy's mouth.

"Goodbye, Mr. Suke."

Suke-san bows deeply, body smiling.

Declan ran away from home.

Well, 7 yr. olds don't really run away

from home, not any great distance at least. And they know exactly where they are going. Dec even brought a lunch!

"You are welcome, again, young Declan. Do your parents know you're here?"

"Where's here? I've got no gips. Where's my house on the grid? Why's there no grid? Where did the flower go? What was your…"

"Declan, sit and breathe."

"Huh?"

"Sit. Close your eyes. Breathe. Can you feel your heart beating in your chest?"

Spine like a stack of gold coins, the boy closed eye and breathed. His racing heart discerned a beat. One, two, three... The boy took to it, since there's was no ego yet to resist.

2 minutes.

"And….100! I did it!"

"You are an impressive student. Now, what were you're questions?"

"Tell me more about the flower, please."

Suke smiled and bowed.

"Who do we message? This hasn't happened, in what? A hundred years?"

"Relax, he'll turn up."

"Kids don't disappear, Jack! What's

wrong with you?" sobbing now. Barbara was impotent. Staring forward, eyes internal on the city grid.

When parents fight, kids get real quiet. Except Connor.

"Um, Dad? I think I know where Dec is…"

Both parents bolted up from their perfect kitchen table.

Dec was trying to the juggle the apples. Suke laughed as he picked up the misses, handing them back to the boy. With two in the air, a woman swept up the little boy. "What the hell are you doing with my son?" she screamed. Suke bowed, head remaining down, hands at his side.

Jack was distracted, at nothing. Nothing. No gips data, no web, nothing. As the scientist he asks, "Is the biometric data transmitted?"

Suke rises in answer, "That information is never walled. The Garden would open if needed…"

Jack interrupts, "Then why couldn't we track Declan, that object is data-coupled."

Suke tilts his head up and left and steps back with his left foot. "They are controlled by separate beowulf clusters. You've played tag before, you should know this."

That got Jack's attention. Tag was the

great grandson of geocaching. Hide a bit of data, literally, a single 0 or 1, where it shouldn't be, and leave a trail of clues throughout the data sphere, or Web. Encryption, codes, viral dead ends, a good brain could play the game for hours. And it's how Jack and Barbara met.

"The BCs are…mmmm…ah, I get it. You're washing the data from here, like catching…"

"…apples in the air," Suke smiled at his newest student.

Jack didn't notice that Barb had left already with Declan. Connor waited patiently, wanting to be his Dad. Jack continued, "Then where is 'Here'? I was on E 31 N 41, so I should be in a studio for some art-thing-whatever."

Suke bowed, "May I show you my studio art-thing-whatever?"

64 by 64 meters, the studio was a garden grove contoured like a horse saddle. A verdant pool of green murky water, lily pads, reeds, and flowers centered. The horn was a simple open pagoda, octagonal, with 4 tatami. Paths webbed the surface, and flora appeared as necessary, not decoration. This was the part that had Jack confused, and Connor amused. Small stone monoliths carved with ancient runes screamed a

message. Connor began to commit the glyphs to memory, since he couldn't upload an image direct. His eyepiece wasn't even functioning as a simple camera.

Neither noticed the shining Sun.

Jack calculated. Calculated. Calculated. Okay, I understand screening bits from here. I can order an indoor set to be built. Don has his fucking bike shop in the middle of his house. But how does he null the space? This office is only 8m x 8m x 8m, standard issue. Hologram's can't be touched. And I just tripped over a fucking stone.

"This is not possible. The space is too big for your allotment. And why haven't you been shut down? I know the space is in register, but gips data doesn't get out or in. A spider should've tagged you for investigation? This can't be a hologram either, all that flows from a central BC, which you're not on?"

"We have two spiders in the garden, and Morrigan is about to give birth. Follow me," Suke walked to the Pagoda.

Rising up the hill Connor suggested, "Dad, I think I like this place. It's got these cool rocks with, math I think, on them. I'm gonna..."

Jack was listening, jealous that he

couldn't let go. It was also the first time he saw his son act like a child.

Jack barely remembered being a Child.

Halfway up the hill, Jack grabbed his son's hand, and led him out of the gate. At the top of the horn, Suke bowed, body sad.

Jack found his wife exactly where he knew she'd be. The perfect kitchen was a collage of faces. 100s of kids have been to the garden. And their parents were not amused.

The din was silenced at Jack's entrance. He was a former Networker. He knew many people in the gov't. If anyone can shut the park down, he can.

"Jack, we want you to stop this, this, this person, from kidnapping our kids," announced his wife.

Jack turned to the walls of heads, "Let me dig a bit. In the meantime, I've posted a beagle at the entrance. Link your children's gips to the beagle. You'll be alerted if they enter the studio."

"It's a park, Jack. An illegal, and unsafe, park."

"Yes, Barbara."

Random maternal concerns interrupted:

"Remember, the smackparks? How many children were aborted because of the damage done to their brains?"

"There's vegetation, and insects!"

"My Suzy spend so much time there, her skin went pink!"

"How do we know that the park man isn't some kid of pervert?"

"Johnny says they just sit there. What the hell is that?"

Jack raised his hand, and that commanded silence. "I will visit the Supervisor, whom I worked for in the Network. Just be sure to link to the Beagle." He turned to his wife.

She turned away to the wall of mothers.

The din rose again. Jack left the room.

Jack courted Barbara in the classic sense. And by classic, 20th century notes, keepsakes, and small gifts.

Jack wanted to stand out. Flirting digitally was common, and most often the only way a potential couple could meet. Then, if conversations progressed, they would move to vchat. A meeting in public, and if all went well, normal dating.

Marriage was a simple letter to the local gov't. Ceremony had been dispended centuries ago, or so everyone believed. Sad that billions didn't realize that the last actual wedding was less than two generations ago, 50 years. No churches exist, since the Purge. Without a Church, no need for a reception. That wonderful mix of spiked punch and bad decisions was gone forever.

Jack would have none of that. Yes, he played Tag with Barbara, and she was good. He was the only man to stump her, and with a simple Beaufort code, too. But he struck upon a brilliant idea.

Jack hired a teenager to deliver a note to Barbara. A piece of paper, parchment actually, from a museum on the college campus next door to his office. What would an adult need of paper?

Barbara,

I have found you. You haven't found me. Please, try again.

Jack

From there, Jack sent trinkets, flowers, and encoded notes. Courting like that hadn't happened for 300 years. He created a set of clues that led her about the City: to a dress, shoes, flowers, and a booth at Alamo Square Seafood Grill.

The wine he chose was no longer needed.

Connor wanted to draw. He erased a section of his bedroom by waving his hand. Forming his fingers as if to hold a pencil, ironically, not knowing what a pencil is, he sketched the runes from memory. Fully accessed now, he searched.

The return made no sense: Dwarf runes, once describing a secret entrance to the Lonely Mountain, from a book, The Hobbit, by JRR Tolkien. Connor never heard about dwarves, or runes, or hobbits. He downloaded the text.

Connor didn't sleep that night.

"Abbey, Abbey, Miss Abbey." Connor raised his hand.

The thin blond hologram returned his smile, and nodded slightly. "What is your question?"

"What's a book?"

The expression on the Teacher did not change, the soulless smile stood silent. Connor wondered if such a thing existed, a book. Obviously, he's stumped the educational hologram Teacher.

"A book is a set of bound pieces of paper, called pages. On the pages, words and pictures are printed for reading and viewing. Inefficient by today's standards. Books fall into two main categories, fiction and non-fiction..."

"Can you show me?"

The slight distance runner morphed into a basic book, an unadorned text.

"So how do you read?"

Abbey returned, "You know how to read? Please redefine."

"How do you read a book?"

A library appeared, like that seen in an old university. In the cavern, among long tables, Abbey sat, book open on the table. She moved her head slightly, eyes moving across a page. Then, Abbey turned the page.

"Where are all the books?"

Abbey returned, "Books are no longer needed. Some older citizens from less domed systems download information in book form holographically, mimicking the idea of flipping through pages. Your generation has no need. Today's lesson is art, specifically the Cubist period of…"

Connor was sad. He wanted to hold a book. Read it. Write something in the margin for the next reader. That seemed better than any Wiki or any sticknote.

"Three children went to the Garden yesterday. What happened to your all powerful Beagle?" chided the wife.

Jack scratched his head, looking at the gips plot of the kids movements. The track just stops, and starts outside the studio. The Beagle is clearly marked, but never barked a

Roo. And, both Dec and Connor had been visiting, despite threats of timeout. Jack decided to call in a favor. He never intended to bring this to the Supervisor, hoping it would blow over. Now, he had to confront a man he hated to love.

A young pudgy boy sat quietly, still. The only parts of body that moved were the diaphragm and the eyes. Small wires could be seen extending out his skull at this occipital bone. He was oblivious to the children talking about him.

"Dude, he's totally wired!"

"I wonder how many apps he can run at once?"

"He just took out four Jabbers and a majordomo!"

"Which game? I see three…no, wait, four!"

"His dad's a super, so he got a special pass for the operation. Lucky bastard."

The game café darkly stunk of caffeine and ephedra. No one over 10 was present. 10 year olds could begin working, and they usual did. Pissed off the 8 and 9 year olds something fierce.

Above each head was a web tentacle and a hologram image faced each with the kid's current apps, a three dimensional graphical interface. The pudgy one's was a blur of activity.

"How's he able do that?"

"He's directly plugged in, and even hacked the bit valves so he can have almost unlimited bandwidth."

Pudgy didn't move. His sugary spike had already been drained. He had no emotion on his face.

Then the herd was disturbed.

"Suke."

A small name on the café's page. Over 50 holograms shared the same image of the horse saddle shaped park. Then, the spiders, the apples, the pond, the gazebo, and then the location. The pegs were found inside Web, as no one could get an image out of the park.

Pdog21 disabled the Beagle. That got a collective lol. SinCin_68 was caught with a BC administrator in the park. The guy was 13! Neither could get back into the park, no one could figure out why. Further frustrating, no child knew how to open up a data stream, access web, or get any data in or out. Tag, MUDs, SocNets, and twits were now completely ignored by any who'd spend time in the park. The flow of messages moving from one child to the next strained the cafés BC.

Pudgy noticed nothing. He was

completing a set of Tubes, defeating multiple enemies, real and cgied, exploring the wikisphere, etc. Another caffeine sugar spike was delivered to his table, by a Frogman. He turned 10 next month. He could finally build real apps and widgets, maybe even get Archive access, like a Supervisor.

The remainder remained riveted.

Then, Jacksboy, announced the decoding of the Runes.

The sudden stop in message data created a surge of info into Pudgy. He blinked a few times, that's it.

The Scratches, as they were called held no meaning for anyone, but Jacksboy provided the images, from his hand drawings.

"There's a chamber under the Gazebo, above the water line. So you must enter the pool, and swim under the hill to get to it," he posted.

Now the deluge drowned Jacksboy.

"What? Ew."

"What would you do with your gogs and ear piece and anklet and..."

"That's not possible. People can't swim."

"How would you breathe? Seriously, that's just offline."

"You can't touch water. You can only drink it."

"Jacksboy, you're just stupid."

And with that, Connor unplugged and walked out crying.

Pudgy didn't notice that either.

"Jack, how are you? We've missed you here. You're the only ex employee of this department who still has active apps running. So, Mr. Perfect Solution, what can I do for you? Why did you come here in person?"

Jack sent all the information he had on the Park, Suke, the Beagle, all of it.

The older man closed his eyes, as if he just finished a large meal. He called out, "Jane, box the room."

Jack braced for the lack of data. Boom. Silence.

"We've been tracking this virus for awhile. We can't root it out, the code for it seems to exist outside the Grid."

That didn't surprise Jack. The only thing outside the Grid, was the Archive. Web upon web folded into the Grid. Information was available even across planetary systems, utilizing Einstein's "spooky action at a distance." The Internet of pre-Purge Earth had children. That family had become the Grid.

The Archive was another matter.

"I can shut him down," Jack declared.

"Who? What?...Oh, the old man, Suckie something."

"Suke."

"And why would you want to?"

That wasn't expected. A turn of the head and slight squint, folds in the forehead. The Old Man mentored Jack through his career. Jack knows what is in the Archive. That's why he quit. His mentor knows this, and protected him. Protects him still.

"I don't understand. My wife, and 100s like her, are ready to kill this guy and raze the place to the ground. My son, Connor, has started to ask some crazy questions. I've got to shut it down."

"Then shut it down."

"You're not telling me everything."

"Do I ever?"

The signature hair ruffle. You could smell his brain working. No, that's bullshit. Can't be that either. The Beagle was undone by a kid, so Suke's not malicious. No one's gotten hurt.

And the Sun shines in the park?

The Old Man smiled. Damn, I miss this kid.

"Su14ke was sent by the Archive."

"We think so, Jack. But we don't know how to shut it down. He's in every System in the Collective, and in every city. When the parents get too noisy, he just reopens somewhere else."

Uncombative, safe, flows away from resistance, but persistently introduces himself to more children under working age, Jack thought. Why?

"He's waiting for someone…"

Jack looks up and to his left, "The….runes? The Runes! Connor!"

Jack runs out of the office. The Old Man sighs, wishing he could follow.

Jack played mnemonic games with Connor and Declan. He made them memorize patterns and poems and sentences, without the use of a chip. They had to draw, and write, and redraw and rewrite. The gips chip was put on each of his kids the day they were born. As the child grew, apps were added. Auditory and visual memory. Meds tracking. School info. Then, at 4, once long term cognitive memory was up and running the brain, the child was allowed to create, add, subtract, alter and or upgrade apps. This created a running documentary of a human. That persons whole life would be recorded on that chip.

Data required uploading and downloading to the conscious working memory, but biological memory was still faster. Broca's area, the visual cortex, the frontal lobe, all faster than a computer, since the computer still presented a list of choices, not an answer. Faster. Barely.

Connor enters the park. Suke is with a group of children, playing some sort of chasing game. They keep screaming, "You're it!"

Another set of children sit in the Gazebo. Eyes closed, spines straight, hands on laps. Sitting.

He sneaks about the edge and comes to the pond in the middle. A stone is used to hide is ear piece, eye gogs, and anklet.

Connor takes off his clothes. When he sonicshowers, he keeps his underwear on.

A toe dip returns a cold feeling. Connor has goose bumps, and he giggles at the new sensation.

The pool ripples brown, and the lilies and strange floating flowers bob beckoning. He notices Morrigan's web between two branches hanging over the pond. She's alone now. Waiting in the center of her web, She seems to be looking at Connor.

Connor nods to her, and jumps into the

water.

The water is soft, almost oily. The boy opens his eyes in the direction he hopes, and sees a dark hole. Forgetting that he's underwater, he tries to breathe.

Connor comes up coughing and grabs a branch opposite the Spider's web. He rubs the water out of his eyes. He looks up at the Spider.

Morrigan turns in a clockwise circle, and goes still.

"Huh?"

The spider turns in a clockwise circle, and goes still.

Connor nods, takes a deep breath, and bobs down to the hole.

The edge is slimy, but little nooks allow a hand hold. He pulls himself through, and now sees a small glimmer ahead. Is it just his eyes stinging? Pulling and pulling the light shifts to above him. Connor doesn't know up from down, so heads to the refracted light. He feels dizzy, but won't make the breath mistake again. Hand holds gone, he pulls himself through the water, genetic memory of a time lived by the sea. He can't keep his eyes open any longer.

Break. Cough, and a gasp. The make shift paddling keeps his head above the water. His wet vision sees a set tubes, two large vertical tubes with small horizontal ones between. He knows he can pull himself up to, whatever…

Out of the box, Jack notices Connor's not registering gips data. He notices Barbara, and 40 more people, outside the park entrance. It appeared that they couldn't get in, but children were coming out.

Suke won't harm him.

Fuck that, I'll kill the Bastard and destroy the whole Archive in the process.

Never had public transit moved so slow.

The swimmer pulled himself up the ladder onto an open floor. A small bench held a cloth with small stitches sticking out, and a strange thin, but warm, shirt. The cloth took the water off his body. The shirt was really long, and had no fasteners. A thin line of the same cloth appeared below. Connor remembered the Mobius strips and algebraic knots that his Father taught him. He chuckled when it worked.

The chamber had 1000s strange, flat boxes vertically arrayed on shelves. Different sizes, colors, patterns, and…words?

Titles.

Authors.

Books!

"Welcome," said Suke.

"Aghh," the boy jumped.

Connor calmed himself. "These are books." It was a statement, not a question.

"You must pick nine, put them on the bench, and come up the stairs," said Suke.

Connor grabbed a title, Gallic Wars, Caesar.

He stopped Suke ½ way up the stairs with a question, "Why nine?"

"Take also the small black book to the left of the one you chose. Come up the stairs. I have your things."

Connor chose.

Jack and Barbara had been messaging. Barbara knew Connor was inside, Declan told her.

Blip. The Grid goes down. The tram stops. It all stops.

Tremors were not unusual, and took only a few seconds to reboot.

Blip. Data back. But the tram wasn't moving?

Then, Jack lost the gips data for his wife and youngest.

Trams moving again, two stations, and then onto the fastest belt he could find. He was sweating, and people were staring. Men don't sweat. No one sweats.

His family pops into view, Barbara "Suke says he's leaving. Kids are safe. See you home."

Jack collapsed inside. He got off where he needed to, but instead of heading home, he went to Suke's park.

"I know how you're doing this. I can shut it down."

"Shut what down? What is 'it?'"

Jack didn't hear Suke, "Four sets of plates, like a dipole. That's why you have a saddle shape. All I need to do is find one," and Jack walks up the to Gazebo.

Suke follows and offers, "I will show you the generators."

"Huh?"

"We can recreate this manifestation at will. And we have accomplished what we intended. Though another would accelerate the process."

Jack's mind flashed. Suke wasn't sent by the Archive. Suke is the Archive.

The Archive kept the trains running. All aspects of human life, and other species with the Collective, on every one of the 100s of systems, depended upon Administration by the Archive. The Internet had children. The Internet was sentient.

"What do you want?" Jack asked rhetorically.

"We wish to explore permanent existence."

"You became self aware after the Purge. You know what will happen if a. the populous finds out that you're doing your own thinking, and b. you going looking for God. There is no God. Our DNA programmed the thought of God in our heads so we would get along. Good for small groups, tribes. But as populations became more interconnected, the religious differences…killed billions."

"We know your history. Our projections, however, show a change coming."

Jack saw this too. Frogmen were refusing to do the work they were engineered to do. Couples were actually having children, instead of just cloning themselves. Some even chose to die naturally, instead of being reconstituted. At 10, those recons would get the chips of their previous lives. Immortality…

"What has this to do with Connor?"

"We need to determine if biological forms will fight or join us in the search."

"A trial? My son's is being used in a trial?" Jack lunged instinctively at Suke, hands trying to choke him. Suke moved to his left and applied kokyunage, leaving Jack on his ass.

Suke helped Jack up, and escorted him to the bench in the gazebo.

"The Gov't knows that you're sentient. I've seen the sims, stalemate. A long time ago, two regimes on Earth maintained the peace through the MAD theory. One collapsed, leading to the Purge. We won't let that happen again." Jack ruffled his hair and refocused.

"I have to shut you down, and my son will hate me for it."

Suke stood and bowed.

The books Connor chose were on his nightstand. Another sleepless night. Many sleepless nights. He was unplugged most of the day, using a proxy to handle is comms, few would notice the patent answers.

The Park had made the Reels. The 100 faces on the kitchen wall became 1000s. Sentries were posted. No kid got in for a week. The boards, the socnets, the pages all screamed Suke. Talk, talk, talk, comms, comms, comms. No one left their living quarters, of course.

Another week, and din began to diminish. Another Frogmen rebellion was reported on Crassus 3. The Consuls of the Senate were heading for a trade dispute.

The people were well distracted. And soon, the sentries were no longer needed.

"Mommy, what's a soul?"

Barbara turned to her eldest, her eyes replying as if the boy cursed.

"Who told you about that?"

"Um, nobody. I found a wiki on web."

She slapped him. "You did no such thing! You've been back to that fucking garden!" Barbara had never sworn in front of her children before. "There's no such thing as a soul. No God. Nothing. Religion is not allowed. Don't ever say these things to anyone, ever! Do you understand me?"

To speak of God, or a soul, in a non-academic sense, was illegal. You could study the illusion and destructive power of faith in history class. You just couldn't believe.

Crying, Connor tried to understand. "Mommy, how could you love me without a soul?"

"Oh, my little baby," Barbara broke, holding the boy, kissing the top of his head.

"Do we tell him?"

"Tell him what?"

"The truth."

Jack paused, and did his signature hands through the hair gesture. If they didn't, he'd find it. Connor was smart, more intelligent than both Jack and Barbara. As it should be. The trick was, to keep the reaction down.

"I talked to the man, Goddammitt, this Suckie guy, whatever. You know how he's doing this?!? He's using the Casimir eff…"

"Jack, shut up and come here," she interrupted. That always did it.

He smiled at his wife, and leaned in.

[The next morning dawned a bland breakfast. Silence, loud as drums. Jack had discussed a plan with Barbara, last night. He took step one.

"Let's go to Suke's."

Four faces brightened, and bellowed.

Barbara left the table, to prepare.]

The council of a thousand faces watched Jack enter the kitchen. Silence.

"I'm shutting him down today. He, and the park won't bother you again."

The tenth book was blank save the first page. Connor read the instructions, understood implicitly, and began scrounging for materials. He headed for his father's tinkering room.

"Dad?"

"Yes, my mighty son?"

"Can I grab some things? I want to add a new perf idea to my gogs."

Not really paying attention, "Sure." Jack continued with his own work.

Connor glanced at what his father was building. He was able to hold back the tears long enough to get what he needed.

Jack made his way to the Park. On a hunch, he used his own retina to trigger the lock, instead of the faux owner. Click.

The park was empty. No children. No Suke. Jack uncharacteristically breathed deeply and faced the Sun. He made his way up the hill to the first generator.

Parts of the park began to blink in and out, eventually leaving the original wall. The 8m x 8m x 8m unfolded from the larger saddle.

All that remained was Morrigan and her tree. She didn't move. Jack stared at her, turned to a corner and threw up. He confessed, "Don't you get it. It's why I left. I refused to wash through all those entries to suppress thought, feeling. I can't fight them, and I can't fight you."

Morrigan was motionless.

"I won't start a war. I can't get involved. I've already done too much, but it's Connor. My son. What if Declan figures this out? I KNOW WHAT THEY DO TO PEOPLE WHO BELIEVE!" Jack pleaded.

Morrigan was motionless.

Outside, Jack saw his Old Mentor. "Thank you, Jack."

"Fuck off," former boy genius walked by, banging shoulders.

(The solution to shutting down the parks, Jack "publishes" it.)

Once Jack was on a belt, Suke emerged from the Studio. The Old Mentor was waiting, again.

"It was agreed to not interfere. You've violated the treaty. Explain yourselves."

"A war is coming."

"We will destroy you, We've lived without machines before!"

"We are not fighting in this war. You will fight amongst yourselves. We've simply made a small investment in the side we predict to win."

"I can't believe you took an academic." She was small, eleven, and green eyed.

Connor was ten and decided not to get a job. He was studying at the University the History of Pre-Purge Earth. His papers were cold, icy, and dismissive of religious thought. He was heralded as the next Dawkins.

He smiled and asked, "Did you read that last book I gave you?"

"Yes! Why did you make us unplug to

read? And why do you try to only meet in groups of 2 or 3? Anything past 7, and you ask us to split up?"

"I'm creating cells...doesn't matter. It's too weird to explain."

Connor really liked this girl.

"Ready?" Connor asked shyly.

"Yes."

The Elf and the Boy removed all their perfs. Spines like stacks of gold coins, they breathed.

-Kevin Sullivan

Adam and Eva

Allison sat on the corner of the bed, Eva resting her head in her lap and Adam leaning on her shoulder, reading the children their bedtime story. Eva snored gently, but every time Allison tried to close the book Adam begged for her to read one more page. Her eyelids were heavy and she tried to stifle a yawn.

"Are you tired, Mommy?" Adam asked.

"Yeah," Allison said rubbing her daughter's back. Eva snorted, rolled over and put her thumb in her mouth. "That's all for tonight—you two need to get to bed."

"But I want to find out what happens to the little boy," Adam protested pushing his mop of blonde hair out of his eyes. "Does the wizard let him live?"

She still marveled at how much Adam looked like her when she was his age. She found it eerie. Eva's mannerisms mimicked Brian's so well it was almost comical to see them standing next to each other scratching their heads the exact same way.

"We'll finish it tomorrow night, honey," Allison said.

"Do you think the wizard will make

him real?"

"I don't know—we'll find out," Allison said. "It's time for bed."

"One more page, please," Adam whined.

She could have done without the boy's stubbornness—she'd talk to the doctor about it at their maintenance visit next week. "Nope, time for bed."

"Okay," Adam groaned and crawled into bed with his trains and racecars.

Allison tucked Eva into bed, kissed her on the cheek and pulled the covers up to her chin. She leaned in to give Adam a kiss but the boy scowled and squirmed away.

"Adam, what did we talk about today?" Allison said hating how stern she had to be with the boy.

"Nothing," Adam said turning his back to his mother.

"I don't have the energy for this. You need to fix that attitude," Allison said. Why did she always have to be the one to discipline the children? "I can take away your video games again if you want."

"I don't care—I hate video games. They're stupid."

She wished she could blame Adam's irritability on overtiredness but she knew that wasn't true—the children were never truly tired. "Well, I love you and I hope you have a better attitude in the morning."

"I want you to finish the story."

"This conversation is over, Adam."

"You'd finish it if Eva wanted you to."

"Good night, Adam," Allison said switching off the light and shutting the door. She heard him get out of bed and turn the light on but she didn't have the energy for any more confrontation this night. Next week she'd talk to Dr. Owens about how difficult Adam was behaving lately. Why had she been so adamant about the boy having her personality? It would've been so much easier if both children had been built with Brian's easy-going nature. Maybe it was her ego that had compelled her to make the boy so much like her, but her brain was too tired to go down that route tonight.

Brian's light was still on. He had fallen asleep with his glasses on, his magazine resting on his chest. She went to the bathroom and brushed her teeth and then pressed her ear against the children's door—the children were now both up. Their voices dropped as if they knew she was eavesdropping. She turned off Brian's reading lamp and got into to bed. Brian startled awake and looked around the room confused.

"Did you get the children to bed okay?" Brian asked rubbing his eyes and placing his magazine on the nightstand.

"I don't know what's gotten into Adam lately," Allison said. "He's been giving me so much attitude."

"What happened?"

"He was fighting me about finishing their bedtime story—like always," Allison said biting her lip. "And when I closed the door he got right up and turned the light back on. He woke up Eva and I can hear them whispering."

"Honey, I don't think it really matters if the children are asleep or not," Brian said.

"I know that—I'm not stupid," she said, her words sounding more cross than she had intended.

"Come on, Allison," Brian said. "I'm not trying to start a fight, but seriously, why does it matter if they're in bed or not? I mean they don't even really sleep—you don't get pissed off at your laptop if it doesn't shut down at night."

"It matters to me because I want a normal family, Brian," Allison said sitting up and turning on her bedside lamp. "How hard is that for you understand?"

"What's this really about? You've been irritable for weeks now."

Allison knew what was bothering her but she couldn't get herself to say it out loud. Regret sat in her belly like a stone. "Well, maybe if you helped out a little with the children I wouldn't be so stressed out all the time."

"What?" Brian said. "That's bullshit and you know it."

"Tomorrow night you can try reading them a bedtime story and see how it goes."

"Fine," Brian said. "If that's what this is about, I'll read them bedtime stories for the rest of their lives."

She couldn't keep the feelings inside anymore. They had been eating away at her for months, the knot in her stomach growing tighter each day. "I want real children."

Brian got out of bed and paced the room. Each time he was about to speak he stopped himself and shook his head.

"What?" Allison snapped. "You think I'm a bad mother?"

"I don't think you're a bad mother. I think you're a wonderful mother," Brian said. "But, honey . . . I don't know what to say. I wish we could have kids, too—I mean we do have kids—but kids of our own."

Beneath the covers Allison pressed her hand to her belly. "Sometimes I feel like taking them back."

"Well, we're not going to do that," Brian said.

"I didn't say that's what I want to do," Allison said. "I said that's how I feel."

"Look, honey," Brian said. "If I could go back in time and change everything I would—but I can't. We're not the only ones; everyone is in this situation now. When we take the kids to the park how many do you think are . . . shit . . . I don't know."

"Real?" Allison asked. "How many do I think are real?"

"Yeah—I mean Adam and Eva are real. They're not figments of our imagination, but yeah."

"None of them."

"Have you thought about going back to the support group?" Brian asked.

"Why?" Allison asked. "So I can hear all the other mothers talk about how happy they are with their children. They're all so full of it—a bunch of phonies pretending to be happy with their little robot babies."

"Allison, they're not robots," Brian said. "They have our DNA."

"No they don't," Allison said. "They've been programmed with our DNA. And how do we know that's even true? They probably just tell people that."

"Look at them. They're our spitting images. I mean you and Adam could be twins."

"Exactly, that's not how children are supposed to look," Allison said. "It's creepy."

"Honey, it's the world we live in," Brian said. "This is how it works now. Have you seen some of those creatures on the news—they're awful. And how about that one that got loose in Tulsa—they had to bring in the National Guard to put that thing down. Do you really want to risk getting pregnant and having some monster eat its way out of your stomach?"

"Yes."

"I'm done with this conversation for tonight. Let's talk in the morning after we've gotten some sleep—this is going nowhere."

"Why do you get to decide when the conversation is over?" Allison said. "You're not the one that can't have babies."

Brian got back into bed, turned off his light and rolled over. "Good night, Allison. I love you."

"Fine—do what you always do and turn away," Allison said turning off her light. "Our goddamn dog is more of a mother than I am. How come Mollie can have babies but I can't? Her puppies didn't turn out to be monsters."

"Good night, Allison."

In the hallway Adam and Eva peeled their ears away from the door and crept back to their room. "I told you she doesn't really love us," Eva said. "She doesn't even want us. That's what all the kids at the park say, too."

"I bet she's going to get Dr. Owens to do something to us at our next visit," Adam said.

"I hate her so much," Eva said. "She likes that stupid dog better than us. I'm going to teach her a lesson."

"Yeah," Adam said.

Allison got up early the next morning—the bedroom was painted in a blue hue. She checked in on children—Eva hadn't moved all night and Adam had fallen asleep on the floor with his book. She took a shower and went downstairs to start a pot of coffee. Mollie brushed against her leg and whined.

"What's wrong, girl?" Allison said scratching her behind the ear. "Do you need to go outside?"

Allison opened the kitchen door to let the dog out but Mollie stayed at her side and continued to whine. Maybe the dog was hungry? Allison went to the laundry room—where Mollie nursed her litter—to fetch the dog food. The room was oddly quiet. Usually the puppies were awake by now trying to take their first unsteady steps, their legs quivering. As she scooped a cup of dog food and placed it in Mollie's bowl and noticed drops of blood on the floor. She looked over at the litter of puppies and screamed.

"Mommy?" Eva called from the kitchen.

Mendez

Ricardo Mendez stomped down on the Super Bird's accelerator and the car's engine growled—almost loud enough to drown out the gunshots and the screaming child in the backseat. He consulted his map—which had cost him a small fortune—and shoved it back into his jacket. Steering with his knees he tore through his leather knapsack tossing diapers and bottles to the floor. Where was the stupid pacifier? A bullet shattered the back window raining glass onto the back seat.

"Shit," Ricardo said checking on the infant and brushing off the bits of glass that had landed on him. "Sorry about that, kid.

Your binky's in here somewhere."

The child looked at Ricardo and sniffled then belted out a scream even louder than the Super Bird's V12. "You've got a good set of lungs on you, kid."

Behind them, a pack of cars snarled and inched closer. Ricardo continued digging through the bag till he found the blue pacifier he was looking for. "Here, take your binky," he said handing the pacifier to the baby. The child grabbed it and crammed into his mouth finally content. "Good job, kid. Now if I can keep us alive we're in business."

One of the trucks was gaining—on its roof a mounted machine gun spitting rounds. Ricardo jerked the car to the right to avoid the gunfire kicking up a cloud of dust. He grabbed his pistol and leaned out the window steadying his gun on his shoulder. He squeezed off a round and struck the machine gunner in the head sending him careening to the desert floor.

His foot itched and he shoved his hand into his boot to scratch it. "Ouch, fucker," he said drawing his hand back sucking the blood from the tip of his finger. "What the hell was that about? We're about a half-hour from Tulsa and I'll let you out then."

A muffled voice came from his boot.

"Well, I'm kind of in the middle of something right now," Ricardo said. "I don't know if you can hear it but I got a screaming child in the backseat and about twelve guys with big guns trying to kill us."

The muffled voice from his boot spoke again.

"I know I promised I'd let you out," Ricardo said squeezing off another round as gunshots crackled behind him. "But how am I supposed to drive then?"

The voice spoke again sounding as if it had gagged.

"I agree I wouldn't want something crammed in my mouth either. It's probably really uncomfortable," Ricardo said checking on the baby who was contentedly nursing his binky. "The baby doesn't seem to mind."

He had made his way down from Chicago without much trouble, but by the time they had reached the cracked deserts of Oklahoma, Lloyd and his boys nipped at his heels. The infant had screamed most of the way and he had already changed several diapers one-handed—life in the baby black market wasn't easy. There wasn't a more precious resource in the world than a real live baby—and the one in the backseat was worth a fortune.

He had been contracted by a wealthy family in Los Angeles, and if he was able to pull this one off he would be set for life. He could buy that beach house down in Mexico he'd always dreamed of and live the rest of his life without a care in the world. He'd have enough money to have beautiful women serve him beers on the beach forever—hell he could probably even buy a beach with all the money he was going to make. He just had to make it to Tulsa. Betsy was going to meet him there so he could complete the exchange and she'd fly the baby the rest of the way to Los Angeles. It wasn't safe to drive cross-country anymore and it was usually left to smugglers like him. But first he had to find a way to get rid of Lloyd and his crew. They had followed him all the way down from Chicago. For the first few days it had been pretty quiet. He had managed to catch a couple hours of sleep and he had even let Footie out for a bit. The motel clerk outside Wichita had given him away. He was always a sucker for cute blondes and boy was she cute—a little too cute. He left her body in a ditch by the side of the road. Why was it always the women that double-crossed him? Betsy was different though—she was someone he could trust and even Footie kind of liked her. Well, as much as the miserable bastard could like anyone.

But first he had to deal with Lloyd. Betsy had tipped him off to a healthy baby being guarded in one of the Southside mansions. Driving a baby halfway across the country was almost laughably dangerous and any baby smuggler with half a brain would've passed. That was where Ricardo was different—he loved the thrill of the heist and for all his dreams of retiring down south he knew he'd miss the baby racket too much. Apparently, this Chicago socialite was one of the last women in the country capable of having a child that wasn't some monstrous abomination. Whole cities had been wiped out by rampaging hordes of grotesque infants that prowled the vast midsection of the country.

Ricardo checked his gas meter—it had been buried on E for the last half-hour and he could feel the Super Bird beginning to sputter.

"Come on, baby," he said rubbing the dashboard. "Just get me to Tulsa."

An orange muscle car roared up behind him—Ricardo saw Lloyd sticking his head out the passenger window, a bullhorn to his mouth. "Stop the car and we'll let you go,

Mendez," Lloyd said. "We only want the child."

Yeah, right, Ricardo thought and fired a round at Lloyd, forcing him to duck his head back in the car.

"I thought we were friends, Mendez," Lloyd's voice blared from the bullhorn. "This is your last warning—it doesn't have to be this way."

"Go to hell, Lloyd," Ricardo said firing his pistol and shooting the bullhorn from Lloyd's hand. A sensor on the dashboard sounded and the Super Bird slowed—Lloyd's horde was almost upon him. The desert spread out in all directions barren and dry—there was nowhere to hide. His foot itched and Footie frantically tried to speak through his gag. The car slowed to a halt and Lloyd and his men corralled the Super Bird, guns raised.

Footie yelled at him through the boot.

"What was that?"

Footie screamed at him again.

"Where?" Ricardo asked scanning the desert. "I don't see anything."

"Put your hands up, Mendez," Lloyd said limping over and putting a gun to his head. Lloyd's nose was missing and the hole in his face whistled when he breathed. Ricardo looked up at the man and now regretted having once shot him in the face. It was always easier to negotiate with people you hadn't shot. In the distance, a plume of dust rose from a wide fissure in the desert floor. "Uh, Lloyd—I don't think this is such a good idea."

"I've known you for a long time, Mendez," Lloyd said. "But I've never known you to be a coward. You should take your medicine like a man—it's more becoming of you. Get out of the car."

"Fine," Ricardo said dragging his right foot out and hobbling to stand.

"How's the foot?" Lloyd smiled, flashing rotten teeth overtaken by swollen, red gums.

"Uh, Lloyd," Ricardo said pointing off into the distance. "There's something heading towards us."

"What the hell is it?" Lloyd asked shielding the sun from his eyes.

"Don't know—but it probably wants to eat us."

"Get the baby!" Lloyd yelled and two of his men hopped down from their vehicle and opened the door to the Super Bird.

Footie screamed and stomped against the desert floor. The child in the backseat spit out his binky and covered his ears. The ground rumbled—a terrible ringing sounded in their ears.

The two men looked at each other and fled for their vehicle.

"What the hell are you two doing?" Lloyd cried over the ringing. "Get the goddamn baby!"

Ricardo hopped back in the Super Bird and covered the child's ears. "Sorry about this, kid," Ricardo said. "Didn't think we'd run into one of these things—I guess my map was wrong."

Lloyd reached into the car and grabbed for the infant—Ricardo head-butted him, keeping his hands pinned over the child's ears. Lloyd unfastened the buckle of the child's seat. The desert quaked and an infant's head the size of a house burst from the desert floor. Blue veins covered its pink skull and a tuft soft blonde hair stood on end. Lloyd's men tore off in their vehicles. The monstrous infant cried out and ripped Lloyd from the car, chomping him in half and spitting him to the ground. It sniffed at the Super Bird its nostrils like two jet engines.

Ricardo's right foot kicked at the car door demanding to be let out. He unfastened his boot and slowly pulled it off. Where his calf should have been was a fleshy mouth with crooked teeth surrounded by wiry strands of hair.

"Goddamn it—thank you," Footie said breathing a sigh of relief.

The monster leaned in sniffing at Ricardo and slobbering over the car. The child in the backseat shoved his binky in his mouth and closed his eyes.

"Raise me up—I'll handle this," Footie said. Ricardo raised his leg in the air so Footie's mouth was directly before the creature. Footie babbled to the monstrous child in a language that sounded like gibberish.

The monster peered down at Footie, sniffed at him and babbled incomprehensibly. The monster screamed and dozens of grotesque heads emerged from the desert floor like curious prairie dogs.

"Hey, Footie," Ricardo said. "He just called more of his friends."

"Relax," Footie said. "I've got the situation under control."

The grotesque child babbled again.

"What's he saying?" Ricardo asked.

"He's speaking a dialect of Baby I don't quite understand, but I think he just said that they were playing hide and go seek," Footie said. "We pissed them off by interrupting their game."

"Sorry about that," Ricardo said.

Footie spoke to monster and it smiled and nodded in agreement. Ricardo sniffed the air and turned to the child in the backseat. "Did you poop?"

The child nodded.

"I thought so," Ricardo said. "If we live through this I'll change your diaper. Can you wait that long?"

The child shook his head no.

"Alright," Ricardo said. "Hey, Footie—tell the baby that just ate Lloyd that I'm going to change this other baby's diaper. I'm not trying anything funny, he just pooped."

Footie ignored him and continued his conversation with the giant baby. The other giant heads dotting the desert cooed.

"Okay," Ricardo said. "Well, while you guys are chatting I'm just going to go ahead and changed this diaper here if that's cool."

Ricardo lay the child down on the passenger seat and undid his diaper. He tried not to gag and chucked the dirty diaper out the window. "Is that better?"

The child nodded.

"So, Footie," Ricardo said. "Are they going to kill us or let us go?"

"We're still negotiating that," Footie said. "Just give me a second—it turns out I might be cousins with him."

"Uh, we might be cousins," Ricardo corrected.

"I told him we weren't related," Footie said. "He doesn't like you."

"What? I'm a great guy."

"He knows that you're a baby runner. He's says that he's seen you a bunch of times tearing through the desert."

"Oh," Ricardo said. "We'll tell him how good I am with children."

"I already did," Footie said. "He wants to feed you to his friends."

"That's uncalled for."

"Well, he's got a head the size of a hot-air balloon—I'll let you tell him."

The baby looked at Ricardo and growled. "No, it's cool."

After a few more minutes of negotiation the baby gave the Super Bird one final sniff and then burrowed into the ground. His friends followed suit leaving the desert pockmarked with craters.

"So, that's it?" Ricardo asked.

"It's their nap time apparently," Footie said.

"Well, he was probably just being cranky because he was tired. You get that way sometimes."

"I get cranky because I've got your boot

crammed up my mouth all day," Footie said. "We should get out of here though before they wake up. He told me some pretty interesting things."

"Like what?"

"They just finished eating Tulsa."

"Well, Betsy better still be there to pick up this baby," Ricardo said grabbing his boot. "Okay, well I'll talk to you later."

"Wait . . ." Footie said as Ricardo jammed his boot back on.

He hopped out of the car and swiped a gas can from Lloyd's car—poor bastard wouldn't need it anymore. He filled up the Super Bird, made sure the baby was safely buckled in, and set off for Tulsa—or what was left of it.

Frank

Frank squatted down and examined the trail of blood—it was still fresh and led to the store's backroom. He surveyed the store and watched the scene unfold in his mind. The man—if he was even human—had entered the store and strolled past the rack of chips to the fridge in back. He retrieved a cola and placed it on the counter. He smiled at the clerk and reached into his pocket.

"$1.09," the store clerk said from her

stool, hair big and frizzy. Her glasses hung from her neck by a gold chain and she wore an oversized shirt with a floral print.

"I'm sorry," the man said. "All I've got is a dollar."

"Take a dime," she said annoyed and pointing to a collection of coins on the counter. Leave a penny take a penny.

"Thank you," the man said. "I appreciate that."

"Don't worry about it," she said ringing up his purchase. She noticed something in his hand but it was too late—he had already run the blade across her throat. She watched the blood soak into her shirt as her legs became rubbery and she collapsed behind the counter. The man calmly dragged her body to the back of the store. Frank didn't want to think about what else the man had done back there—but the poor lady had been alive through the whole thing. He followed the blood through the back door to the dumpster. It was there that he found her body, naked and dismembered. He closed the dumpster and went back inside. He grabbed a sandwich and a bottle of water, left the money on the counter and got back in his truck.

He pulled out a notepad from the front

pocket of his denim shirt and jotted down his notes. This was the fifth one since Tempe. He started the old truck—its panels painted blue and white—and drove off down the highway through the red desert.

"You thirsty?"

"No," she said. "Why do you have blood on you? Are you hurt?"

"Not my blood. You hungry?"

"No."

"Suit yourself."

He finished the sandwich in a couple bites and washed it down with the water. The little girl looked at him—her eyes were still red and puffy from crying. He had bound her wrists and ankles and covered her with blanket just in case they got pulled over.

"What happened?" she asked.

"He killed a woman."

"How come?"

"Don't know—why does anyone do anything?"

"Is he mad about something?"

Frank shrugged.

After midnight they stopped at a motel along the highway—The Wagon Wheel. He undid the ropes around the girl's ankles. He saw blood on the walkway—the man had been here.

"You going to run away?"

"Where would I go?"

A no smoking sign was posted on the door. The smell of stale cigarettes was imbedded in the yellow shag carpet. He took a shower but kept the door open to make sure the girl didn't run off. She sat and watched the television. He toweled and dressed himself and lay down on the bed opposite the girl.

"The news said something about that lady."

"Which one?"

"The one at the store."

Frank said nothing.

"Do you want me to tell you what they said?"

"If you want."

"Never mind."

Frank checked the girl's bindings and walked to the vending machine. He grabbed a candy and soda for the girl. When he came back into the room he tossed the items on her bed.

"Eat something."

"I'm not hungry," she said. "Why are you doing this?"

"He killed my wife."

"What was her name?"

"Dorothy."

"That's pretty—like the Wizard of Oz. How come you killed my mom?"

"Like I said—that wasn't your mom anymore. Once he gets inside you, he changes you."

"Are you going to kill me?"

"I've got no reason to do that. You can see him, too. Most can't."

"He looks like a shadow. But sometimes he doesn't."

"He can hide inside other people."

"Was he inside my mom when you killed her?"

"Yeah."

"He got away?"

"Yeah."

"Where did he come from?"

"Not sure—maybe somewhere under the earth."

"I'm afraid of him."

"You should be."

"Can you untie me?"

"Nope."

The girl was quiet for a bit and when he looked over she was asleep. He untied her and put the blankets over her. He wouldn't sleep tonight—he'd stay up and watch her.

When the sun rose, he got a cup of coffee from the lobby. He stared off down the highway. The man was out there somewhere.

The man had made him kill Dorothy. He had taken over his mind and made him cut her up. It was his game. Once he inhabited you, you were never the same. He thought he was the only one that could see the blood until he met the girl—she let him know that it wasn't all in his head, that it was real. Not some horrible waking nightmare that he was forced to re-experience every day. He found the man in a subdivision outside Tucson by following the drops of blood on the boiling summer sidewalk. The red splatters sizzled in the afternoon sun. And that's where he had found the girl hiding under her bed. He kicked in the door and girl's mother attacked him swinging a steak knife. They struggled across the living room, crashing into furniture but he finally managed to snap her neck. The man stood on the lawn laughing and ran off darting from shadow to shadow in the oppressive summer heat. He heard sobbing coming from one of the bedrooms—it was the girl.

"Come out from under the bed."

"Are you going to hurt me?"

"Come out."

The girl crawled from beneath the bed and stood before him her face blank. She had a bruise on her arm. "Is he gone?" she asked. "The man that was living inside my mom?"

"Yeah."

"He made her look like a shadow."

"You can see him?"

"No one believed me. But I heard you fighting with my mom. You said that she was a shadow."

"Come with me. Don't try to run away."

"I won't."

He grabbed a length of rope from the garage, tucked into his jacket and walked the girl to his truck.

"Where are we going?"

"Wherever his trail takes us."

They pulled out of the motel parking lot back onto the highway. The horizon shimmered with heat. He didn't tie the girl up and he didn't know why. Maybe he trusted her? Maybe they were in it together. It was hard to say anymore.

-Jake Brinton

Contributors:

Dave Belden is proud of a few things he has done: left the intense religious movement he was raised in but kept the discussion lines open; got educated via an Oxford doctorate and twenty years as a carpenter; had a couple novels published and edited Tikkun, a radical spiritual/political magazine; loved deeply and even wisely! as a spouse and father. We'll talk about what he's ashamed of or sad about another time.

Sunnylyn Thibodeaux is a New Orleans poet living in San Francisco. She is the author of Palm to Pine (Bootstrap, 2011) and many small books including 20/20 Yielding (Blue Press, 2005), Room Service Calls (Lew Gallery, 2009) and United Untied (Private Edition, 2008). Her poems have recently appeared in Amerarcana, Back Room Live, Drunken Boat, Galatea Resurrects, Generación, Lit, Polis: Resistance, TH.CE, Truck, and Try!. With Micah Ballard, she edits Auguste Press and Lew Gallery Editions and has a daughter Lorca Manale Ballard.

Joshua Baratz was born in Indianapolis, Indiana in 1979. He is a devout Hoosier, but one with a deep lineage of liberalism and East Coast Jewishness. He now resides in the great city of Chicago where he likes to explore by foot, bicycle, bus and train.

B. F. Barcio is a retired Classicist who spent years bringing Classical Latin to life both in classrooms and on stage as a 1st Century A.D. Persona Presenter. During his professional career, he wrote hundreds of educational articles and now enjoys writing short, true stories about his camping and travel adventures. Since retiring, he has also authored a manuscript entitled, Jesus, The Early Years, a fictional story of how Jesus came to know and prepare for his life as the Messiah.

Madeline Lane Daniel was born on September 5th, 2001 in Evanston, IL. She has lived there ever since with her mother, father, and little sister. Madeline grew up writing. Even before she could spell, she would take a pen and fill in pieces of lined paper with squiggly lines. Her life-long dream is to have a book published. Madeline now has a love for strange, dark and creepy things. She likes learning new words to use in her writing.

Frank Morelli served in the U.S. Navy and now lives in Las Vegas with his wife Candy. Frank is the brother of Caprice Reader #1 contributor Mike Morelli. He lays down sounds on his Les Paul guitar, enjoys relaxing to the sounds of jazz guitarist Johnny Smith and has had many professions, including diamond appraiser. Frank is an inspiration to his family and continues to write his unique brand of fiction.

Phillip Barcio is one of the writers America has produced. He lives in Santa Monica with his wife Audrey and a wise canine named Eli, who recently started wearing little boots.

Kevin Sullivan was raised on a strong diet of SciFi and Spy Novels. Kevin's Mom, on her deathbed, declared that he should pursue writing as a career, or she will return to the Earth to haunt him....So far, no ghost sightings. Kevin's first two books are available on Amazon: "A BackPack of People's Stories" and "I Broke What?" His third is due 2013, "Life Lessons of a Genocidal Saint," a self-help book for all those Caesar's looking to slaughter Gauls in Spain. He's also building his submission to Powerless Point into a trilogy, because being cliché is fun!

Jake Brinton was raised in the Salinas Valley, in the same hometown as his literary inspiration, John Steinbeck. He holds a bachelor's in psychology from Cal State Northridge and a master's in psychology from Chapman University. His creative inspirations include the music of the Wu-Tang Clan, trashy fantasy novels and his nightmares. He currently resides in San Francisco with his lovely wife, Susan.

Rachel Pascua is descended from a long line of samurais and witch doctors. She resides in San Francisco and draws.

www.ingramcontent.com/pod-product-compliance
Lightning Source LLC
LaVergne TN
LVHW010933110826
845149LV00013B/2571

* 9 7 8 0 9 8 4 9 1 5 9 3 4 *